THE
PRICE
OF EMPIRE

THE
PRICE
OF EMPIRE

J. WILLIAM
FULBRIGHT

with Seth P. Tillman

PANTHEON BOOKS   NEW YORK

Portions of this book are based on speeches delivered by Senator
Fulbright and appear here in somewhat different form.

Library of Congress Cataloging-in-Publication Data

Fulbright, J. William (James William), 1905–
    The price of empire.

Includes index.
    1. United States—Foreign relations—1945–   .
2. United States—Economic conditions—1945–   .
3. World politics—1945–   . I. Tillman, Seth P.
II. Title.
E744.F889   1989   327.73   88-42717
ISBN 0-394-57224-6

CONTENTS

FOREWORD

If I am remembered, I suppose it will be as a dissenter. That was not what I had in mind, but when important issues go contrary to your highest hopes and strongest convictions, there is nothing you can do except dissent—or drop out.

Dissent was not a principle with me. It simply seemed to me that a senator has a responsibility to be independent in his judgments, not just contrary. In a Senate speech back in 1965, following my criticism of the Johnson administration's Dominican intervention, and the resulting controversy, I tried to define the role, as I perceived it, of the chairman of the Foreign Relations Committee. The chairman, I said, "has special obligations to offer the best advice he can on matters of foreign policy; it is an obligation, I believe, which is inherent in the chairmanship, which takes precedence over party loyalty, and which has nothing to do with whether the chairman's views are solicited or desired by people in the executive branch."

Looking back, I recall that my views were seldom solicited by the executive branch—and, I suspect, even less often desired. But I offered them anyway—for better or for worse. What if anything of lasting value I accomplished or contributed is for others to judge. Looking back on a public career that extended from World War II to the mid 1970s, I would say that there were a number of rewarding initiatives—such as the international education exchange program now in its forty-second year, the revival of the League of Nations in the form of the United Nations, to which I believe that I made a modest contribution, and the creation of the Kennedy Center. Sometimes, however, it seems clear in retrospect, I hoped for more than was realistically attainable: I was frustrated by the war in Vietnam and by the resistance to any consideration of a change in the separation-of-powers principle and its presidential-electoral procedure. Like the early Latin American statesman Miranda, who devoted his life to freedom and independence with uncertain result, I am left at times with the feeling that in these areas I "plowed the sea."

Still, I have few regrets, because the paradox of power is that there is relatively little in politics that is readily attainable that is really *worth* attaining. This is not to disparage the dams and river projects, the urban-renewal and farm-support programs that every officeholder supports and promotes. I gladly did my share for cotton, chickens, soybeans, rice, and all the other local industries that have provided a modicum of prosperity to the people of my home state of Arkansas. These domestic programs fall in the category of what is more or less readily attainable. They make life better for many people, and for that reason are eminently worth advancing—but they do not address the larger issues of war and peace in the nuclear age; of the way our nation is governed and the adequacy of that governance for the conditions and challenges of the late twentieth century; of the priorities of national need in matters of security, economy, education, and social justice; of seeing the world as others see it and of progress toward the ever-elusive goal of global cooperation to meet global challenges.

These are what might be called the "survival" issues, and efforts to address them invariably come up against entrenched, traditional modes of thinking, limited vision and moribund imaginations, corporate greed and political ambition, opportunism and demagoguery. In the name of an ersatz "realism," programs for ending the debilitating arms race, for rational reconsideration of our system of government—especially the procedure for choosing the president—or for practical measures toward realizing the unfulfilled promise of the United Nations are, more often than not, dismissed with ridicule and scorn. The epithets change—from "soft on communism" to "gullible," "naïve," and being "against America." Even the word "liberal," derived from the Latin word for liberty, became in the recent campaign a term of opprobrium, shunned by both candidates lest either be thought a defiler of the household gods, a dissenter from cherished old myths, a disturber of the peace that we all find in the familiar and traditional, a challenger of ancient truths that are no longer true even if they once were. When I think of these matters (as I try not to do too often), I am reminded of the words of a Swedish count to his son after the devastation of Europe in the Hundred Years' War: "Remember, my son, with what little wisdom the world is governed." Or I think of a comment of Alexis de Tocqueville in *Democracy in America:* "I know of no country in which there is so little independence of mind and real freedom of discussion as in America."

That is the downside, realistic but despairing, and if it were the only side, there would be little for us to do except await destruction. But there is, I feel certain, another side, a dimension of our human nature, however fragile, that fosters reason and compassion. The all-too-demonstrable fact that we seldom learn from experience does not mean that we *never* learn from experience. Every once in a long while there is something new under the sun—from Periclean Athens to the founding of the American republic, from the long Roman peace to Woodrow Wilson's great conception of world peace in our own time under a regime of law. These are goals worth striving for, and if the past suggests only small hope for success, there is nonetheless a world of difference, and also of promise, between a small hope and no hope at all.

We may indeed be at a historical moment of promise and hope. A number of regional conflicts, including Afghanistan and the Iran-Iraq war, are coming to an end or are in abeyance. A new administration has come to office in the United States, and while it is still untested, the accession of new leaders gives rise at least to the hope of a new manner of thinking. Perhaps most promising of all is the fact of intelligent, innovative new leadership in Russia as well as China, opening what may well be unprecedented possibilities for cooperation to reduce the mutually destructive animosity between the superpowers; for curbing the nuclear arms race and the spread of nuclear weapons; rechanneling the resources thus gained to improving the quality of life in all of our societies; putting in place more effective mechanisms for the peaceful settlement of regional conflicts; and establishing a desperately needed global regime for the protection of our fragile, gravely imperiled global environment.

The historical odds are against us. We, the United States, may go the way of so many great powers of the past—the way of power politics and of mindless rivalry with the other great power, the way of ancient Athens and of the once-mighty, now-fallen European empires of the century past—our once-great promise, the promise of the "city upon a hill," mortgaged and finally sacrificed to the arrogance of power.

But there is nothing foreordained about America's decline and fall. If that should come to pass, it will come because of our own lack of creative imagination, because we remained in thrall to ancient myths and fears when all reason and common sense instructed us to act upon our best hopes and authentic possibilities. The most harmful myth is the belief that there is something sacred about the principle of separation of powers, especially the procedure for the selection of the president. The current practice undermines the strength and credibility of democratic government and is demeaning to the nation.

Our future is not in the stars but in our own minds and hearts. Creative leadership and liberal education, which in fact go together, are the first requirements for a hopeful future for humankind. Fostering these—leadership, learning, and empathy between cultures—was and remains the purpose of the international scholarship program that I was privileged to sponsor in the U.S. Senate over forty years ago. It is a modest program with an immodest aim—the achievement in international affairs of a regime more civilized, rational, and humane than the empty system of power of the past. I believed in that possibility when I began. I still do.

THE
PRICE
OF EMPIRE

1

THE
COLD WAR:
THE U.S.
AND THE U.S.S.R.

As we continue, in the wake of four Reagan-Gorbachev summits, to try to shape a viable policy toward the other superpower, our decisions, I have no doubt, will be based only in part on the facts and merits of special problems, such as the Middle East, the arms race, and human rights. Our decisions will be shaped at least as much—and I suspect more—by the *attitudes* that we and the Russians bring to our continuing interaction. If each side remains, as in the past, basically convinced that the true objective of the other is to dominate or destroy, there will be no comprehensive arms-control agreements, because almost any weapons system is potentially aggressive; there will be no cooperation for peace in the Middle East, because any bid for influence can be read as part of a global design; there will be no sustained increase of trade, because almost any commodity, even food, can contribute to a nation's war-making capacity; and there will surely be no long-term improvement in human rights, because relaxing controls, from the Soviet standpoint, would open the gates to Western subversion.

It is very odd and fascinating to me that we have such an obsession about the Russians. I used to think it was because of communism. But now I don't. I don't think we ever harbored the kind of deep dislike and suspicion of the Chinese that we have of the Russians. Indeed once it became clear to us that the communist leaders of China were as fearful of and hostile to the Soviets as we are, we readily embraced China, communist though it is, as our de facto strategic ally. The Yugoslavs are communists too, and we get along well with them; and we are friendly enough even with the Rumanians. It seems apparent to me now that it is Russia that troubles and preoccupies us. There is something about the Russians that gets under our skin—their size, their power, their credentials as a credible rival for global primacy. In this respect if not in others we and they are alike, and the likeness irritates and offends us.

It is perfectly natural that the United States and the Soviet Union, emerging as the two dominant nations after World War II, fell into rivalry. That has been the way of great powers since Athens and Sparta. It is the age-old game of nations—a cruel and lethal game, to be sure, but a game nonetheless. Ideological differences notwithstanding, war *has* been the game of kings. But nuclear weapons and even the power of conventional weapons have changed all that; it is a new game we are playing in the nuclear age—irrational, inhuman, suicidal—a game with no possible winners, and a game we can avoid losing only by refusing to play.

We deeply feel, it would seem, and sometimes say that we must be number one and, more precisely, must be recognized as a greater nation than the Soviet Union. The issue in its roots is about as significant as who is number one in the football field. We have made global politics into a Superbowl, as if it were something like Nebraska and Oklahoma battling for the title. That's a great thing for Nebraska and Oklahoma, or for the Washington Redskins and the Denver Broncos; their rivalry hurts nobody and entertains everybody. Nor was universal damage done even when France and then Germany vied for the mastery of Europe. But after two world wars, and with the advent of nuclear weapons, that kind of game isn't fun anymore.

I recognize that it is offensive to many—and also to a degree

6

misleading—to describe our contest with the Soviets as a "game": as a contest without moral content or merit. That is not my point. The ideological issue is real and important, as are the strategic and economic stakes of superpower rivalry. But these are not the entirety of the issue, nor, when framed in historical context, is it clear that they are the basic issue. Gamesmanship is the historical constant. It is not *all* there is to great-power rivalry, but it is the element, going back to the Greeks, that always seems to be there, unacknowledged but ever-present.

We are told that the Russians respect only strength. I don't quite know what that phrase, "respect only strength," means. I am not—nor are any of us—advocating that we disarm unilaterally. That is not the question. There is a big difference between aspiring to be number one, with a greater capacity for destruction than anybody, including the Russians, and settling for parity; and that is especially true with nuclear weapons. You have semantic difficulties here, but I don't see that the arms race, in building bigger and better nuclear weapons, increases our security. On the contrary, as Reagan and Gorbachev, by 1988, seemed belatedly to recognize, the arms race in general, and each new advance in weapons technology in particular, has subtracted exponentially from our security.

The threat of the Russians certainly exists, but with nuclear weapons in hand, our whole way of thinking about global politics should have changed. The year 1945 marked a profound break in the thread of human history. In the wake of the two world wars, Europe, hitherto the center of the world's power and culture, lay ruined and demoralized, its preeminence lost—apparently, as it then seemed, beyond retrieval. The Soviet Union had suffered the loss of more than twenty million of its population. China had suffered similarly from both invasion and civil war; and the great cities of Germany and Japan were reduced to ashes. Most of this had taken place even before atomic bombs were dropped on two Japanese cities. The advent of nuclear weapons should have made it abundantly clear—if it were not clear already—that warfare among great nations had become suicidally irrational and therefore intolerable to civilized peoples.

In the face of such great potential catastrophe, the past offers few models for peace and world order, or indeed for any tested system to assure the survival of civilization and human life. Einstein said in 1945, "Now everything has changed except our manner of thinking. Thus we are drifting towards a catastrophe beyond comparison. We shall require a substantially new manner of thinking if mankind is to survive." So far, we have largely failed to achieve this new manner of thinking, and the cost of this failure has been enormous. We are still deeply embedded in a refusal to face the most elementary facts about our situation. We refuse to confront how both we and the Russians have continued to be motivated by obsolete notions of national self-interest and self-aggrandizement. Listening to the Soviet and American leaders talk about foreign policy, you would think nothing could be further from their minds than such preoccupations. Each professes—and in all likelihood sincerely believes himself—to be motivated by the loftiest ideals. Few people are more moved by a moving speech than the speaker himself. But eloquence alone does not define truth. Most of us are deeply attached to our own values and believe in our own superior virtue. But when you look at foreign policy, the generous impulses and ideals professed with all sincerity by political leaders seldom describe, and more commonly obfuscate, their actual policies. We are usually rationalizing our intense competitiveness and self-interest.

Unless we can move beyond this kind of thinking, we have

little chance of successfully confronting many of our shared problems as a species. We Americans are particularly prone to moralizing self-righteousness. By constantly stressing the goodness and purity of our motives, we readily enough conclude that those who question these motives must be moral reprobates. Jimmy Carter's homily of "a government as good as its people" and Reagan's "evil empire" are, in a sense, two sides of the same coin. This is not to suggest that the strictures against communism to which we have been subjected for the last forty or fifty years are without substance. Communism as practiced in the Soviet Union has been in many respects, at least until recently, brutal and tyrannical. Stalin was particularly brutal—a pathological tyrant who, in Milovan Djilas's words, "would destroy nine-tenths of humanity to make happy the one-tenth." Soviet actions in many areas of the world—particularly eastern Europe—have been similarly brutal and crude, although less so in recent years. But there are other aspects to the Soviet system and to Soviet foreign policy, which, weighed in the balance against many excesses, add up to a system that is something less than "the focus of evil in the modern world"—and very much less than the matrix of a vast, global conspiracy.

I have always had difficulties, and still do, in applying the standards of individual morality to the actions of states. The morality of states is different from the morality we expect of individuals, and of necessity less demanding; and although the United States may have a better historical record in this respect than some other countries, we are not generically different from the rest of the pack. Cold-war polemicists like Jeane Kirkpatrick preach about how our moral standards are so much higher than everybody else's, and I have no reason to doubt that they genuinely believe that. Nevertheless, this kind of sanctimony has always struck me as self-serving—and self-deceiving—chauvinism. This idea that everything *we* do is for a noble purpose, while everything the Russians do is a dastardly scheme to dominate the world, is offensive to me. I recall an exchange in the Senate Foreign Relations Committee at the time of the Dominican intervention in 1965 in which one of my Republican colleagues challenged my contention that our military intervention was hardly different from what the Russians did in eastern Europe. I pressed him on what the difference was, and he finally said, "When we do it, it's for their own good." I have encountered this sort of thing—this sense of our superiority—ever since I started in politics, and it has always seemed to me a kind of contempt for other people. We are indeed a good country—a wonderful country in many respects—but I never felt that Americans as such were morally superior to other people. The truth of the matter is that when you look at our actions, as distinct from our loftily expressed self-conceptions, it is difficult to see much difference, for example, between our actions in Vietnam and the Russians' in Afghanistan.

Notwithstanding periodic thaws, arms agreements, and steps toward détente, I think that the great majority of people in this country have been sold on the idea that somehow or other the Russians are absolutely beyond the pale; that, as Dean Acheson once said, it is impossible to do business with them; that there is no question that they are out to destroy us and dominate the world. It is a self-reinforcing approach. There is a psychological condescension towards the Russians in our attitude, as if they were not authentic members of the human race. It is an attitude we don't much bother to examine, but we literally find it hard to see them as respectable members of the human race. I doubt this escapes their notice; it must be very offensive to them. The supposition—not in our regular and routine encounters, nor in our formal diplomatic dealings, but in our bedrock attitudes—is that no matter what they are doing, it is for some sinister purpose.

And they, I expect, reciprocate the image and the perception. The distinguished psychiatrist Erich Fromm wrote in 1956:

The lack of objectivity, as far as foreign nations are concerned, is notorious. From one day to another, another nation is made out to be utterly depraved and fiendish, while one's own nation stands for everything that is good and noble. Every action of the enemy is judged by one standard—every action of oneself by another. Even good deeds by the enemy are considered a sign of particular devilishness, meant to deceive us and the world, while our bad deeds are necessary and justified by our noble goals, which they serve. Indeed, if one examines the relationship between nations, as well as between individuals, one comes to the conclusion that objectivity is the exception, and a greater or lesser degree of narcissistic distortion is the rule.*

I have the feeling—this is very unpopular to say in America, and I'm sure the Senate and the Congress wouldn't accept it—that over the years we have been provocative towards the Russians. We have been provocative in the sense that we have never encouraged them to believe that we accept the legitimacy of their regime, or that we are willing to regard them as political equals within the international community. What our condescension and our moral strictures do encourage them to believe is that our aim is to destroy their form of government; that we want them to become a democracy like us before we will recognize them as equals; that unless they have an elected government like ours, they are illegitimate.

It is in our interests to persuade them that we are not out to undo their government and their system. We might even

*Erich Fromm, *The Art of Loving* (New York: Harper and Row, 1956), p. 20.

admit of the possibility that they are engaged in a difficult but interesting social experiment, and say to them in effect, "We doubt that your system is workable, but if by some chance you can make it work better than we do ours, well, God bless you; but if you don't bother us, don't try to subvert us, then we won't subvert you." I commend such an attitude to our new national leadership, and I recommend too that they find words to express the attitude and actions to match the words.

I became aware of the centrality of this matter of legitimacy when Soviet leader Nikita Khrushchev spoke to an informal meeting of the Senate Foreign Relations Committee in 1959. The State Department had asked me to arrange something for him because, like a priest denying the sacraments to a sinner, the Speaker of the House, John McCormack, refused to let him speak before a joint session of Congress. The same thing happened with Gorbachev in 1987; some of the "conservatives" just weren't going to have a communist addressing them—for fear, perhaps, that the wickedness of so polluting a presence might be contagious. It is ridiculous, of course, especially when you look at the people who have spoken to a joint session over the years, some of whose moral credentials would not easily withstand close examination.

In any case, Khrushchev came to the committee. He spoke with enthusiasm and vigor, and was in fact quite conciliatory. His reputation for bluster notwithstanding, he did not seem very threatening to me. He did not give me the impression he was brooding about, much less plotting, the destruction of the United States or otherwise mapping a game plan for the meticulous execution of Marxian dogma. The heart of his statement was to the effect that future relations between the Soviet Union and the United States depended upon our recognizing that a new society had appeared among the community of nations—meaning, as I heard it, that we should recognize them as a socialist society that had a legitimate right to exist. He did not ask for our approval, just acceptance of the fact. "That in fact is the main thing," he said. We could get along and face the other problems if we recognized their legitimacy.

The old adage says that evil may be in the ear of the hearer. When Khrushchev said, "We will bury you," Americans heard this as a military challenge, a threat of nuclear war, and they were correspondingly outraged. The phrase, to be sure, was provocative, or at least boastful, but during Khrushchev's visit to the United States in 1959, he said with some anger that he had been talking about economic competition. "I'm deeply concerned over these conscious distortions of my thoughts," he said. "I've never mentioned any rockets." Now, in retrospect, why indeed were we so sure that Khrushchev was threatening military destruction instead of peaceful competition? And why, given our own deep belief in the superiority of our system, should we have been alarmed by a challenge to compete?

At times, I think, we harbor a superiority complex: America, in the phrase of John Winthrop that President Reagan so much liked to quote, was "a city upon a hill," a beacon light for humankind. We were created by the greatest instrument, as Gladstone said of the American Constitution, that ever emerged from the brain and purpose of man. We incarnate the self-evident truths of man. What this means in plain language is that we think we are better than anybody else— especially better than those Russians who are daring to challenge us.

At the same time, and paradoxically, we seem afflicted with a kind of paranoid fear of their competition. The highly emotional attacks upon communism and Russia that have become so familiar a part of our national political vocabulary suggest a lack of confidence in our own system's ability to compete effectively and peacefully with the Russians, and especially to do so without utilizing violent oratory to mobilize our people. If these people who profess such profound love for and faith in the American system are as convinced as they say they are, then why are they so afraid—all the more in the face of accumulated evidence that our system *is* more productive, indeed far more productive, than the Soviet communist system?

We talk a lot about being tough, about a tough policy in foreign affairs, about never showing any weakness. President Nixon for one never tired of talking about how tough he was, even when he was making intelligent accommodations with his Soviet counterparts, and none of his successors has failed to take the cue. The premise seems to be that compromise will lead us quickly to the appeasement that begets aggression—an overlearning of the lesson of Munich. In fact, a genuinely strong leader with a belief in himself does not go around trumpeting his virtues and his "toughness." If he has these qualities, they are likely to be self-evident, apparent in actions taken and policies pursued. If he lacks them, bombastic rhetoric will be of little avail. The key question remains whether those extreme ideologues who advocate an ever-escalating arms race, who oppose all compromise, and who never tire of violent language are really as confident of the superiority of our system as they profess to be. They give every evidence of fearing competition on a peaceful basis, and in order to prevent a fair trial in peaceful conditions of our two systems, they try to preempt the issue by engaging the Soviets in an arms contest that will make them go broke before we do. We are to attain this happy outcome by outspending them militarily, forcing them to exhaust their resources, and thus denying them the means either to keep up in arms or to improve their own social conditions. We do have more money, and so far at least we have had the superior technology. The trouble is that, in driving the Soviets towards bankruptcy, we have made alarming progress in that direction ourselves. The game to

14

which our cold-war ideologues have committed us is a losers' game—at least for the players. The winners, present and prospective, are the bystanders, in Europe and Asia, whose resources are committed to making their own societies work.

What, indeed, are the Russians really like? Can we conceive that they share with us a common human nature despite differences of culture and political tradition? Is it possible that their motives, like our own, are often ambiguous and obscure, to themselves as well as to others? Is it true—or still true—as Dean Acheson told the Senate Foreign Relations Committee in 1947, that "it is a mistake to believe that you can, at any time, sit down with the Russians and solve problems or questions"?

After forty years of almost constant interaction, we have still not fully made up our minds what the Russians are really like. During these decades two schools of thought have competed for the allegiance of the public and congressional opinion. The more influential has been the cold-war school, which remains wedded to the belief that the Soviet Union is driven by ideological zealotry, that its internal practices are incorrigibly repressive except when outside pressure is applied, and that, despite tactical concessions from time to time, the Soviet Union can never be anything but an inveterate antagonist to the United States in world affairs.

The other school of thought—the détente school—basing its observations on Soviet *behavior* rather than doctrine, contends that, at least since Stalin's time, Soviet foreign policy has been pragmatic rather than messianic, opportunistic but not universally predatory, and that on the basis of its actual performance the Soviet Union has shown itself to be a generally reliable collaborator with the United States in honoring the terms of existing arms-control agreements, keeping the lid on

15

regional conflicts, and paying its commercial debts. As to Soviet internal practices, the détente school has held that these
are for the most part beyond the reach of foreign influence,
but in any case more amenable to influence through improved
relations than through pressure.

Despite doubts cast by the Gorbachev era of *glasnost* and
perestroika, the cold-war school has largely dominated American views of Russia since shortly after World War II. It is
perhaps best enshrined in the Truman Doctrine and in NSC-
68, a 1950 document prepared by members of the State and
Defense departments. "The Soviet Union," said NSC-68,
"unlike previous aspirants to hegemony, is animated by a new
fanatic faith, antithetical to our own, and seeks to impose its
authority over the rest of the world." The choice faced by
nearly every nation, as President Truman defined it in his
famous address of March 12, 1947, is that they "must choose
between alternative ways of life," the one based on democratic
institutions like our own, the other based on "terror and
oppression."

Couched in these terms, the choice would have seemed easy
and obvious. But our postwar policy-makers perceived the
Soviet Union as possessing a diabolical magnetism for its prospective victims. During the heyday of McCarthyism in the late
1940s and early 1950s, the Russians were credited with an
uncanny ability to subvert free societies, including our own,
through the manipulation of gullible idealists. As the hysteria
mounted, the category of gullible idealist was broadened to
include—and besmirch—almost any public person who
thought it possible, and worthwhile, to try to cooperate with
the Soviet Union in specific areas of our relations.

The philosophy of the Truman Doctrine has largely held
sway and exerts a profound influence over our policy to the
present day. Only occasionally has it given way to the détente
school of thought at several crucial junctures over the years:

under President Eisenhower, when hesitant efforts were made to reach an understanding with Khrushchev; under President Kennedy, when the nuclear-test-ban treaty was concluded; most significantly, under President Nixon and Secretary of State Kissinger; and most recently and interestingly, under President Reagan in his final months in office.

Overshadowed though it has been, the détente school of thought, I believe, offers a more accurate—and surely more promising—perspective for future Russian-American relations. Evaluating Soviet intentions on the basis of performance, rather than the worst-case scenarios so beloved of our strategic planners, the advocates of détente look to both the past and the future.

In the past they see that, since the early postwar years, when the Russians established their domination over eastern Europe, the Soviet Union has not engaged in overt military aggression beyond its sphere of influence over eastern Europe—with the single, major exception of Afghanistan. There the Soviet leaders intervened not, I think, as part of a great design to envelop the Persian Gulf and threaten the free world's oil supply, but in panic at the imminent collapse of a Marxist client.

All but the most unreconstructed cold-warriors now recognize that the Vietnam War was not part of a Soviet world design, but was essentially a civil war in which the Soviet Union supported one faction while we, on an incomparably greater scale, supported the other. Still looking to the past, advocates of détente note that the Russians have shown a continuing interest in strategic-arms limitations and in trade, and that when agreements have been reached they have for the most part honored them.

Looking to the future, I do not foresee perfect harmony or an end to competition between the superpowers, even in the warm afterglow of the Reagan-Gorbachev détente. What I do

17

hope for is a somewhat more explicit agreement on the rules of competition; a certain number of cooperative agreements, of which arms control, based on the purported acceptance of parity, is the most important; increasing communication and contact on many levels, including, especially, educational exchange; and a reduction in the intensity of the mistrust that poisons our relations.

Perhaps something exists in our Puritan heritage which causes us to feel that if we cannot have perfect harmony, we do not want it at all. Instead of treating our various dealings with Russia as simply problems to be solved, we have tended throughout the history of the cold war to approach each encounter as a new morality play. This sorting of the good guys from the scoundrels may be mordant fun for moral crusaders, but its uses are quite limited—and so, too, are its moral dividends.

I do not know—or much care—whether the Russians' motives are idealistic or opportunistic, as long as they behave and act in ways that allow us to cooperate. Nor am I prepared to excommunicate them from the human race if they cooperate on one occasion and then turn up as our rivals on another. I think it is imperative to seek out those areas of cooperation wherever they can be found and build upon them to whatever extent is possible.

Assaults upon the merits of détente with the Russians are not only inflammatory but sterile. They are sterile because the critics of détente seem to assume that there is a satisfactory alternative to Soviet-American cooperation, when in fact the only alternative is the cold war and its endless polemics, the ruinous arms race, and periodic trips to the nuclear brink. It may well be granted that Soviet-American cooperation has been less than might have been desired in innumerable situations, but does it follow that we would have been better off with no attempt at cooperation at all? The burden of proof has repeatedly been placed on the wrong side. Instead of holding the advocates of détente to an exacting, if not impossible, standard, the detractors ought to be required to show that they have something better to offer.

Early on in these forty-plus years of superpower rivalry, we stopped thinking about what the Russians might be *likely* to do and focused instead on what they could conceivably do if they were inspired by an irresistible determination to destroy us. It is part of the illogical cold-war psychology that still to a great extent burdens us. In this perspective, Russians are guilty until proven innocent—or guilty simply by definition. The hard-liners, instead of being expected to show how a Soviet proposal might be part of their devious plot to gain supremacy—or for that matter, how Nicaragua, or Vietnam, or countless other situations, might be part of a plan to communize or dominate the world—so manipulated our national dialogue in the postwar years as to be able to demand that the skeptics prove that Soviet aims were in fact benign. If the skeptics could not—as they usually could not—then we must continue on the assumption that the worst-case scenario was the accurate one. Otherwise we would be recklessly endangering national security. It is the ultimate illogic: to maintain that the arms race is the course of prudence; that confrontation is the mark of courage; that Vietnam, Nicaragua, Grenada, and so on, are merely defensive, conservative responses.

You cannot deal with the Soviets this way and hope to resolve anything, much less stabilize the international system. You cannot know what is going on in their minds with any certainty. You cannot deal with them on the basis of their presumed intentions. You have to respond to people on the basis of their observable actions and behavior, and place the

19

burden of proof where it belongs—on those who assert and accuse rather than on those who question and raise doubts. These are the most elementary rules for ascertaining truth; it is the essence of the surviving tyranny of the cold-war ethos that we still cannot see this.

Acceptance of the cold-war ethos has repeatedly led, in the case of strategic-arms-limitations questions, to an obsessive preoccupation with what the Russians might do under agreements we might make with them. We try to imagine all the various ways the Russians might cheat, and come up with all sorts of dizzying calculations as to what they might do under this or that provision of some potential agreement. In the midst of these Byzantine calculations, the most critical strategic issue facing us and the Russians is lost sight of: What will we do—what indeed will become of us—if we cannot reach any comprehensive agreements to limit and radically reduce the costly striving for nuclear superiority?

I don't expect our competition with the Russians to subside in the third-world countries, much as I wish it would. They have not given up the idea of extending their influence, and I don't expect them to for a long time. But I don't think the United States is going to give up its idea of trying to promote its way of life for a long time, either. Both of these great powers are engaging, in reality, in quite similar activities in third-world countries to promote their ideas of how to organize society.

There is nothing new in this. Great powers have been doing it throughout history. The Spanish excuse was that they were going to convert the heathen and save their souls from hell. That was all a fraud. I don't know if they sold anybody but themselves, but their excuse for their barbarous activities was to pretend they were doing the Lord's work. It's much the same today with the Russians and us. The human race and the great powers remain afflicted with these fantasies.

Looked at from the Russian viewpoint, it might readily appear that we by and large *bought* the allegiance of much of the world in the early postwar years. They couldn't match the expenditures we made. They only had recourse to other methods—those of subversion and the use of local communist parties, which didn't cost as much. In Egypt they did send in the equivalent of billions of dollars, though without much effect in the long run. Because we had lots of money in those days, we could send aid all around the world to gain the support and allegiance of various countries. The Russians always accused us of this, and in looking back, there is some truth in the accusation. That is, in part, how we got so many votes on our side in the United Nations. We could usually win on any question because we had the votes of the Latin American nations and all those others to whom we gave such generous subsidies.

We have given far more aid than the Russians have. Why did we do it? Was it pure altruism, or did we do it to expand our sphere of influence, to attract the support of the beneficiaries in the United Nations, and to allow us to trade with them with all the privileges of a big friend? Of course, it was in our perceived self-interest, and the Russians had the same idea, lacking only the means. Although I do not think that it is in general accurate, I have no difficulty understanding how the Soviets, given their ideology and their historic security fears, could believe that the vast amounts of money expended by the United States on some thirty or forty countries in the early postwar days, under such programs as the Marshall plan, was part of a great design to incorporate these nations under our economic control.

Of course, there is a difference between what we have done and military aggression aimed at direct control, as in the Soviet invasion of Afghanistan. Nevertheless, we have used other means to maintain our strategic and economic

interests. Our outrage at what has happened in Central
America—notably in Guatemala in 1954 and later in Cuba—
was in no small measure related to the expropriation of
American property. We have not wanted to directly incorporate these nations into the United States, but we have
wanted to have a dominant economic influence over them.
The Russians are a little more primitive, as in Afghanistan
and in eastern Europe. Physical control is the old, traditional, colonial way. The British profited greatly from it; but
it has become unacceptable and untenable in modern times.
The Russians have only recently shown signs that they have
begun to learn that lesson; recognizing that they made a serious mistake putting their troops into Afghanistan, they decided in 1988 to withdraw them. We cannot, however, be
too sanctimonious about Afghanistan, because what we did
in Vietnam was not wholly dissimilar. Only Vietnam was
much farther away; we had in reality nothing to fear from
what was happening there. Afghanistan is on the Soviet border and they might have had some legitimate concern, if not
fear, that the dynamism of the fundamentalist Islamic revolution in Iran could spread not only into Afghanistan but
also into their own Muslim-populated border regions. It is
plausible that they could have rationalized it this way, although I hasten to add that I don't approve of what they did;
there was no excuse for it.

The issue in any case is not approval but empathy. We seem
to have great difficulty putting ourselves into the position of
the Russians to see how they might look at us. On various
occasions over the years I have suggested that Soviet concern
with our overseas bases was not an unreasonable obsession.
Many were located within short range of them. They had
deterrent value, we were quite confident, but that did not
preclude them from appearing offensive and provocative to

the Russians. Did we try to understand that? Did we make allowances for that in our refusal to consider any negotiation over the years about those bases?

Or again, I think this refusal to look at ourselves as the Russians might look at us and then to act with this awareness in mind may have contributed to the Soviet willingness, if not the decision in December 1979, to invade Afghanistan. It came after Carter's peremptory rejection of a proposal by Brezhnev to discuss their reducing conventional forces in central Europe in return for our not putting intermediate-range missiles in western Europe. Carter made an offensive speech in response—saying, in effect, that it was all a trick, that Brezhnev was trying to fool the American people and the Europeans by this phony offer to negotiate. I should have thought it would make more sense to say, in effect: "OK, let's negotiate and see what you'll do. You say you'll withdraw a thousand tanks, but be serious about it. Were you to withdraw five thousand, in return we would do something comparable, such as not putting in certain weapons," and so on. In other words, the proper, responsible response to an offer to negotiate is to negotiate and see if the tensions can't be lowered. That is the only way that an unfavorable status quo is going to be altered; it is not going to be altered by more weapons and more military expenditure.

I have no way of knowing whether the Soviet proposal was serious or not; nor will we ever know—because it was not tested. I do think that provocative reactions to Soviet initiatives are likely to result in their feeling that they have nothing to gain by conciliatory offers, that they are not going to make any headway with America, so they might as well go ahead and do the things their hard-liners advocate. I can see how, in weighing the dangers from Muslim fundamentalism and turmoil in Afghanistan, they could finally come down to saying,

"Let's take care of Afghanistan, since we will really lose nothing with the Americans."

Now these are in part psychological considerations. How do you evaluate intentions, how do you see them being shaped? If we make a conciliatory gesture, how might they respond?

In the past it seemed that every time it looked as though we might be able to improve Soviet-American relations, something unusual happened. The U-2, the death of Kennedy, the shooting down of the Korean airliner at the time of the nuclear-freeze movement, Watergate—all destroyed any movement toward détente or arms control. It is difficult for me to accept the idea that such occurrences are *always* coincidental. I can't prove anything, of course; I only have suspicions. Truman once commented that every time we started to make progress with the Russians, something seemed to happen. He had the idea that there were forces around who just did not like the idea of our having normal relations with the Russians. Even granting that these disruptive events have been coincidental, they have certainly been seized upon by those among us—they call themselves "conservatives"—who believe that the Russians are the devil incarnate and that to compromise or have anything to do with them is a mortal sin.

It is the presence of people in government who will take almost any steps to thwart détente or normal relations that fuels the kind of popular suspicion that surfaces when something like the downing of the Korean Airlines plane occurs. It is still a great mystery to me why the pilot was not warned he was off course. Is it possible he was not warned because we hoped to gain some intelligence advantage as the plane flew over Soviet military bases?

We will probably never know for sure either what happened with the U-2, which destroyed the promising movement towards détente back in 1960, when Khrushchev was going all out to improve relations. I believe that Eisenhower really was interested in establishing normal relations with the Russians. He less than others felt the paranoia that has afflicted so many postwar American leaders. Khrushchev's visit to the U.S. in 1959 had been a momentous first step. And in Paris, where Eisenhower and Khrushchev were scheduled to meet in May 1960, they were apparently going to agree upon a visit by Eisenhower to the Soviet Union. I even heard rumors that they were building a golf course outside of Moscow expressly for Eisenhower.

Eisenhower took responsibility for the U-2, and that action destroyed the summit conference. It would have been wiser if he had said that there was a miscarriage of policy, that he had not personally or specifically authorized the U-2 flight or intended to violate Soviet airspace. From a personal point of view, taking that responsibility was an admirable act, but from a political and national perspective it was mistaken and unfortunate—a classic example of how moral standards that are properly applicable to individuals can be disruptive, in some instances, when applied as acts of state. Eisenhower's acknowledgment of responsibility left Khrushchev with no way out of an embarrassing political bind. He could have overlooked the episode and gone on with the meeting if Eisenhower had denied responsibility. I think Khrushchev clearly wanted—even encouraged—Eisenhower to say that he really didn't know about this particular flight, that it was a regrettable miscalculation.

But instead he took responsibility and compounded the insult by asserting that we had a right to overfly Soviet territory, partly because the Russians are so secretive. That was obviously unacceptable to Khrushchev, and it led to a very serious setback in our relations. Khrushchev at that time was on the defensive with his own people for having tried to promote good relations with the United States, his own hard-liners being rather like our own in their affinity for devil theories of the opposition. Furthermore, it was unprecedented for a chief of state to assume personal responsibility for covert intelligence operations. The deliberate and intentional assertion by Eisenhower that he had the right to violate the territorial sovereignty of another state could only be considered an extremely unfriendly act of the utmost seriousness. To say that Khrushchev used the U-2 to wreck the conference, as was argued at the time, was hardly an accurate view of the situation. We forced him to wreck it by our own ineptitude.

The Foreign Relations Committee held extended closed-door hearings in 1960 on the U-2 incident. There was suspicion at the time that the incident had been deliberately timed by the CIA and some of its operatives. You would think that if we were serious about negotiations, we would have suspended the flights just prior to a superpower summit. It was inexcusable to take the chance of having a spy plane shot down at so crucial a moment. Of course, the flights had been going on for some time, and it is possible that the failure to suspend them was not malice but simply neglect and incompetence. My surmise is that Eisenhower was generally aware of the flights, but not necessarily of this particular one. My guess is that if he had been aware of this particular flight at this particular time, he would have said, "Don't do it until we get through with the meeting." He was a sensible man. It's ironic—he probably could have disavowed responsibility and been telling the truth.

But to have handled it the way we did was most unfortunate. Suppose it had been the other way around, I suggested at the time. Suppose a Soviet counterpart of the U-2 had come down over Kansas City. Just imagine the thundering outrage and vociferous speeches in the Senate, denouncing Soviet perfidy on the eve of the summit and proclaiming that the president should certainly not go to Paris. Then imagine how much more violent the reaction if Khrushchev had said he was personally responsible for it—and at the same time left the impression that he had every intention of doing it again, and that he was entirely right to do so.

It was a great and costly loss to both nations. The failure of the Paris summit of May 1960 probably contributed to Khrushchev's unwise and rash decision to install missiles in Cuba, of which the consequences in turn contributed to his dismissal and the adoption of a whole new approach by a new, more orthodox Soviet leadership. Khrushchev was discredited in the eyes of his colleagues and domestic opponents, and the idea that normal relations could be established with the United States was discredited in the Kremlin.

There followed a period of no progress at all. The competitiveness became more intense than ever during the Kennedy administration. Kennedy in his campaign for the presidency in 1960 used the alleged "missile gap" as a major theme in his contest with Richard Nixon, a contest in which both candidates pulled out all the stops of cold-war rhetoric. Ironically, it is probable that this mistaken allegation, followed by the Bay of Pigs fiasco and a contentious Kennedy-Khrushchev summit at Vienna in July 1961, incited the Russians subsequently to increase their arms program. The outlook of the time was expressed by Kennedy in his first State of the Union message, when, speaking of Russia and China, he said, "We must never be lulled into believing that either power has yielded its ambitions for world domination—ambitions which they forcefully restated only a short time ago."

In this frame of mind we increased our commitment in Vietnam. Too prudent to challenge the Russians directly, but too suspicious to try to cooperate with them, we chose instead to engage them—and the Chinese—along the periphery. We would show them—so we thought—that they could not conquer the world through "wars of national liberation," just as we had shown Stalin that he could not do it by "direct" aggression in Europe.

For a brief moment in the summer of 1963, I hoped Soviet-American relations could improve. Having looked down the abyss, as it is said, at the time of the Cuban missile crisis in October 1962, Kennedy and Khrushchev abruptly changed course. At American University in June 1963, Kennedy made the most enlightened and conciliatory speech about the Soviet Union made by any president up to that time. The American University speech created a favorable atmosphere for the negotiation of the limited nuclear test-ban treaty, which was signed in August 1963. I went to Moscow for the signing of the treaty. Khrushchev was there, very friendly and agreeable. Kennedy's speech and the treaty had created a promising new atmosphere. I would like to think that President Kennedy would have gone further in that direction, and specifically that he would not have escalated the war in Vietnam. I'd like to think that, but I don't know. Khrushchev, for his part, was showing considerable courage in his de-Stalinization campaign, as well as in his efforts, over the opposition of Kremlin hard-line conservatives, to ameliorate the tension with the United States.

It was just a brief moment. Kennedy was murdered in November 1963, Khrushchev was removed from office in October 1964, and the Johnson administration fell—or plunged—into the maelstrom of Vietnam. It's strange how fate in that sense plays such an enormous part in the history of countries. It's not that Lyndon Johnson did not wish to reach some agreement with the Russians, but with the rapid intensification of the war in Vietnam, prospects for détente largely collapsed, and stayed that way until Nixon became president.

I thoroughly approved of what Nixon did in his relations with China and Russia. It came as quite a surprise to me.

I believe that the general approach of Nixon's détente policy was, and still is, in the interests of the U.S. and the U.S.S.R. The prospects were briefly hopeful. In the year 1972 alone, more substantive Soviet-American agreements were signed than in all the years since diplomatic relations had been established in 1933. Following upon the Moscow agreement of May 1972, agreements were concluded in Washington in June 1973 for cooperation in oceanography, transportation, agricultural research, and atomic energy, as well as for the establishment of direct airline service between the two countries, expanded cultural exchange, and the extension of credits for the construction of a large fertilizer complex in Russia. In addition, a declaration of principles for the prevention of nuclear war was issued, and guidelines were laid down for the negotiations then underway on strategic-arms limitations known as SALT II. There was even a little-known joint undertaking to study and revise school textbooks used in each country with a view to making them more accurate and generally reducing the demonizing tendencies on each side with regard to the other. This small but felicitous initiative, with its special significance for influencing the perceptions of coming generations, was canceled by President Carter after the invasion of Afghanistan in an act more accurately characterized as self-punishing spite than as meaningful retaliation.

By far the most important agreement to date for détente is the ABM treaty of 1972. Under this agreement, which limited each power to no more than two—later reduced to one—antiballistic-missile sites, the two nations, in effect, have committed themselves to permanent coexistence. Insofar as each side abandons the effort to make itself invulnerable to attack or retaliation, it also commits itself to peace and to the survival of the other's power and ideology. That is the essential meaning and value of the ABM treaty, and it is precisely that which President Reagan tried to undercut with his fantasy of impregnable defense under the so-called Strategic Defense Initiative.

Nixon's efforts to create détente with the Russians were very important. I did my best to encourage him in this direction because I thought, on this most important subject, he was right. When he returned from the 1972 Moscow summit he briefed the congressional leadership at the White House; it was one of the ablest presentations I had seen. Nixon had a grasp of détente's significance.

Kissinger did too, or so it seemed at the time, but he doesn't seem to support the idea anymore. He can make you believe that he is on your side. I didn't know until much later that he had the capacity to do this to people with diametrically opposed views. Some of my Democratic colleagues suggested at the time that I was being taken in. Perhaps so, but I failed then—I fail now—to see the logic of withholding support for a program I had long advocated, just because it was being advanced by Republicans.

When Watergate broke, progress toward détente ended. The Foreign Relations Committee investigated Kissinger's role and I thought Kissinger was probably involved in lying about the wiretapping. Many of the top administration figures were being challenged and disgraced. The feeling in the Foreign Relations Committee about Kissinger was, what good does it do to just put another scalp on the shelf? We didn't cover anything up. We just didn't conduct a lot of hearings and go all out to prove that he was lying. My impression then was that he was, but so were others connected with the issue. I didn't think it useful to pursue it. There was so much scandal, and I saw no useful purpose in publicizing more. I for one was particularly concerned that the preoccupation with Watergate—the moralizing and recriminations, deserved though it may have been—was incapacitating the nation's leadership, distracting the nation from serious policy matters, and providing an opportunity for the ever-eager enemies of détente.

And so it did. Watergate destroyed both Nixon and détente. Later many said that détente had failed. In fact it was never tried. It was sabotaged especially by Senator Henry Jackson, whose infamous amendment proved an utter fiasco with respect to its ostensible purpose—freeing up Jewish emigration from the Soviet Union—but a sterling success with regard to its real purpose, which was sabotaging the Nixon détente. I don't consider that it's a failure of détente when an external force like Henry Jackson intervenes to destroy it. If it had been tried, and we had attempted to live up to it, and the Russians had violated it, then I would have said it failed. But it didn't work out that way.

It is true that Nixon's policy, which was originally approved by Congress, eventually lost that support; but I believe it lost support for causes quite irrelevant to the validity of the process initiated and the agreements made at that time. The failure of Nixon's détente policy was essentially a product of the circumstances of Watergate, itself a product of the disastrous Vietnam War, which together undermined the power and prestige of Nixon's administration. The gratuitous injection of the issue of Russian emigration politics into the 1974 trade bill aborted that promising measure, which was to have implemented a Soviet-American trade agreement and, incidentally, a settlement of the World War II Lend-Lease debt.

It wasn't the Russians who exploited Watergate to the detriment of our foreign policy, but certain of our own military leaders and certain members of the Senate. From their perspective, Nixon's conception of "shared goals of coexistence" was a dangerous delusion. The Russians, once again, were seen as bent on world conquest, using détente as a trick or a tactic towards that goal. Watergate unleashed once again these cold-warriors in the Pentagon and the Congress to launch a highly effective, concerted campaign against arms control and trade with the Soviet Union.

I did not believe then, or now, that the human-rights issue in the guise of the Jackson amendment should be allowed to stand in the way of getting something done in the area of arms control or trade. It is perfectly legitimate to encourage the Soviet Union to relent in such areas as Jewish emigration, but I see neither merit nor relevance in the denial of equal-trade treatment as a sanction for that purpose. It was in any case counterproductive. Before the adoption of the Jackson amendment, the emigration of Jews from the Soviet Union had reached a high of almost 35,000 in 1973. Following its adoption in 1974 emigration fell to 15,000 in each of the years 1975 and 1976. At the same time, other avenues to improve relations were effectively aborted—and that, I strongly suspect, was the real purpose of Senator Jackson's venture into the field of "human rights."

Détente was too fragile to withstand repeated American provocations of the stolid, suspicious Soviet leadership. We have talked about Soviet aims repeatedly in an insulting manner. It is true, of course, that they do not conform to our concept of human rights, and some of their past practices have not conformed to anybody's concept. When it comes to physical repression, no one can approve of some of the things they have done. The question, however, is whether using human rights as a weapon of cold-war diplomacy is effective. It is also relevant to note—though the point is not easily made in our ethnocentric American political culture—that the emphasis we place on the right to criticize and condemn the government, to engage in acrimonious internal discussion, is not considered a fundamental human right in many societies. I refer not only to the Soviet Union. Neither the Japanese nor the Chinese, among a great many societies, share our preference for clamorous political dispute.

In any case, if we could reduce the burden of the arms race and the mutual militarization of our economies, I think the atmosphere for human rights would be greatly improved. We would certainly get a different sense of which societies function best.

Closely related to this is the question of actual differences between socialism and capitalism, and of how we are to understand these differences. I personally believe that our economic system, which stresses personal incentive, is more closely attuned to human nature than the egalitarianism of Marxist doctrine. But we tend to overlook the fact that our social and political system was established upon probably the richest, most productive, most desirable piece of real estate in the world. If our system had been implanted on the bleak areas of Siberia, I doubt it would have been so productive. I think it possible too, though heretical, that a socialist system in the United States would be prosperous too—perhaps less productive overall, but with a higher degree of social justice and equality. The relevant policy question, however, is not which system is better, nor which would work better under hypothetical conditions of equal resources. The key question is the willingness of both sides to engage in peaceful competition—to put ideology to the only test that counts, the test of which system can produce a better life for its people.

I think we could win that competition—though in that kind of competition there are no real losers—because fundamentally our system is more in accord with human nature than the socialist system, whose practitioners tend to expect too much of it. For all their excesses and even brutality in practice, the traditional ideologues who have ruled the Soviet Union were in a fundamental sense too idealistic with regard to the capacity of man to work for the common good. I don't think most people will; they work for their own gain, which can have fallout for the common good. That is the quite evident premise of Gorbachev's *perestroika*. If foreign pressures lessen, the Soviet leaders may become more flexible. The centralization of decision-making in Russia could be relaxed, and while the Soviet leaders would continue to profess their ideology, they would adopt pragmatic measures that would enable them to introduce economic incentives even though these are not in accord with the fundamental dogmas of socialism. That is what other countries have done. We, on our part, though capitalist, do many things that are socialistic in nature, involving government interference in private enterprise—such as the TVA, Amtrak, and Conrail.

Those dogmatic distinctions don't appeal to me. What does appeal to me—and that more deeply than I can easily find words to express—is the idea that if we could eliminate the arms race, we would have the opportunity to see which of these societies really does function best.

The centerpiece of détente—if there is to be détente—is the control of strategic arms. Nixon clearly saw this. Its importance, however, though obvious to ordinary people, sometimes seems to escape the experts, and therefore bears repeating: arms control is important because the leaders of the Soviet Union and the United States have the means at their disposal at any time to destroy each other's cities and much or most of each other's populations. It is theoretically possible to prevent war by maintaining a strategic balance in an uncontrolled arms race, and it is even possible, theoretically, to limit the arms race by voluntary, unilateral restraints on the development of superfluous weapons systems. Recent experience suggests, however, that to the arms experts there is no such thing as a superfluous weapons system, and all history—from antiquity to the world wars of the twentieth century—shows that peace cannot survive indefinitely on the basis of fear alone. It is an accepted principle of psychology that fear shapes behavior; our prophecies tend to be self-fulfilling, so that if we live in the constant expectation of war, we will probably, in due course, get it.

Attitudes are consequently very important. But how do you deal with the Russians? By negotiations, I should think: by working with them, by joint ventures in a growing number of areas. This is what Nixon began to do before détente collapsed in the early 1970s. We ought to follow up on these initiatives—as perhaps, unexpectedly, we were beginning to do in the last months of the Reagan administration. The critical element is that in our direct relationship we develop a measure of confidence that we can cooperate on the basic issues we face in common. Over time, joint ventures can help us develop a sense that we can work together—a feeling and a belief on each side that the other is not going to resort to force to establish its domination.

Unless we take measures to generate a growing confidence in our ability to work together, the danger of war will remain—notwithstanding *glasnost, perestroika,* summit meetings, and the INF treaty. We could be drawn into a conflict by quarreling clients, especially in the Middle East, in the pattern of World War I. It is essential, therefore, that a sufficient degree of confidence be established so that both of us are willing and comfortable about calling the other one up on the hotline and saying, "Look, let's talk it over before we go any further." That is an oversimplification of what I think is the right approach, but implementing the principle involved is the only kind of hope we really have for a peaceful, secure future for humankind.

Throughout most of his administration, Reagan quite evidently disapproved of this kind of thinking. He said several times that if SDI worked, we would give it to the world. Perhaps President Reagan was quite sincere about this, but I cannot easily conjure up a vision of Pentagon hard-liners and right-wing zealots graciously instructing Soviet counterparts in the technology of "Star Wars." In any case, if Reagan did mean it, why did he not invite the Russians to join in the actual research, to participate in a joint venture to see what actually could be done with lasers, with particle beams and all those exotic weapons, to join us in their development? That might have been credible, and I suspect the Russians—once they got past their initial incredulity—would have been quite reassured. But the way Reagan put it was all a fraud. Nobody believed we were going to share anything.

When it comes to keeping treaties, I don't think the Soviet record is any worse than ours. You can't trust any great power to do what it doesn't want to do, solemn commitments notwithstanding, and I can't say we can trust the Russians—but I can't say they can trust us either. Consider what we have done in Latin America. The Bay of Pigs in 1961, and the intervention in the Dominican Republic in 1965, to cite only two conspicuous examples, were blatant violations of the charter of the Organization of American States. We ignored our treaty obligations and did as we pleased. We paid no attention then, and we pay no attention now when treaties and promises get in our way. In my experience this isn't the kind of topic you discuss much with your fellow senators, who in private react as though you're a little naïve to bring it up. It always puzzled me, however, that the same senators who thought me naïve for objecting to *our* treaty violations would be seized with moral indignation at real and alleged Soviet violations.

I once had the Library of Congress review the question of Soviet treaty compliance. They reported that by and large the Soviets honored their agreements when they dealt with specific contractual obligations such as money payments, or other clear and specific commitments. It was when you got into general ideological engagements—those George Kennan calls "declaratory," such as the clauses in the Helsinki treaty about freedom and democracy—that the situation was quite different.

Allegations in the last few years of Soviet violations of the ABM treaty are very hard to pin down. Such Pentagon hardliners as Richard Perle, Henry Jackson's protégé, who became an assistant secretary of defense in the Reagan administration, made a mighty uproar about the Soviet radar installation at Krasnoyarsk, but when some congressmen went there, they found its real purpose unclear. They could not tell whether the installation was designed just to trace satellites or whether it might actually be used to shoot down incoming missiles. The congressmen concluded, in any case, that it was not a significant affair.

Previously, our government accused the Russians of supplying and prompting their friends to use poison gas in Cambodia and Afghanistan. It turned out that the "yellow rain" that was said to be evidence of the poison gas in fact came from the feces of bees. The episode would seem to constitute another example of the Reagan administration's penchant for "disinformation"—which is a polite word for lying. The trouble with this kind of misrepresentation, of course, aside from any moral scruples it may tax, is that once a government becomes suspect as to its truthfulness, it can neither lie successfully nor hope to be believed when it is telling the truth.

37

The way the Reagan administration tried to reinterpret 1972 ABM, for example, was truly irresponsible. I was floor manager of the ABM treaty in the Senate in 1972, and I can testify for a certainty that the reinterpretation offered in 1987 by the Reagan administration's State Department legal adviser, Abraham Sofaer, was a piece of legal and intellectual legerdemain, running directly contrary to both the Nixon administration's and the Senate's understanding of the treaty as ratified. Under the terms of the treaty, the Reagan administration had the option to offer an amendment to alter the treaty. But lacking the votes to do that, they tried, with strained and devious reasoning, to change the basic meaning of the treaty.

When the treaty was debated and overwhelmingly approved in 1972, neither its proponents nor opponents, nor those who had reservations but in the end voted for it, supposed that the treaty contemplated or would permit the development and testing of antiballistic weapons in space. The radical reinterpretation of the treaty proposed by the Reagan administration, so as to sanction SDI, ran directly counter to the plain language of the treaty, to the intent of the Nixon administration as it was explained to us at the time, and to the clear understanding of the Senate.

Had I suspected at the time that the ABM treaty could validly be interpreted so as to allow for Star Wars or anything resembling it, I would either have opposed it or proposed a clarifying reservation or interpretation. I certainly would not have guided it through the Foreign Relations Committee and sponsored it as a floor manager.

The ABM treaty codified the central strategic reality of the nuclear age: that neither we nor the Russians have, or can reasonably be expected to acquire, effective defenses against intercontinental missiles, and that, therefore, there is no useful purpose, and a high destabilizing risk, in trying to build such a defense. That is a sound deterrent principle. It worked, and it still works. The concept enshrined in the ABM treaty was to base the security of both superpowers on mutual deterrence, which is to say, on the certainty of retaliation if either were to launch an attack. It was hoped, too, at the time that the certainty of retaliation would eliminate or greatly reduce the need for costly and redundant offensive systems.

Neither side, it was believed, would start anything provocative—like SDI. No one at the time, to my recollection, ever contemplated the possibility that systems based on technologies not then in existence would be exempt from the treaty's ban on development and testing as well as deployment of antimissile systems. Senator James Buckley of New York voted against the treaty precisely because of this prohibition, saying that it denies us "for all time—or [denies] the Russians, for that matter—the right to protect our civilian populations from nuclear devastation."

Acceptance of mutual vulnerability was the principle of the ABM treaty. That is how it was clearly stated at the time, and you also see it clearly expressed in Nixon's and Kissinger's memoirs. Whatever they may think of SDI today, there is no reason to doubt that, at the time of the signing of the ABM treaty, they regarded the commitment to mutual deterrence as permanent. That is the word used by President Nixon—not as temporary, provisional, or subject to abandonment upon the arrival of some exotic new technology.

President Reagan, as I have said, had the right under the treaty to propose amendments or to withdraw from the treaty. But he did not have the right to perform radical surgery by tortured reinterpretation.

This treaty was clearly made, clearly debated, and there was no excuse for a self-respecting legislative body to give credence to Sofaer's tortured illogic. The Biden amendment to the INF treaty, stating in effect that the Senate has the right to assume that the administration was telling the truth about the meaning of the treaty as submitted to the Senate, does partial compensation for the intellectual and constitutional offense of the Sofaer doctrine.

Whether they represented a real change of heart, or a new appreciation of public-relations opportunities, or simply a recognition of mistakes come home to roost, the policies of the Reagan administration in its last year suggest the possibility of a promising new approach for the new administration.

With enlightened and remarkably audacious leadership in Moscow as a counterpart, our new president has an unprecedented opportunity to negotiate with the Russians on a wide range of issues. Gorbachev offers us an unusual opportunity, and we should seize it before it is too late. The economic foundations of these two military giants are beginning to crumble. The interests that we share as a consequence of our joint responsibilities for world peace as well as of our somewhat comparable economic circumstances offer a real hope of reaching agreements that would free us to deal with our deepening domestic deterioration.

In the last three years, Gorbachev has come forward and demonstrated how dramatically different he is from what we have been accustomed to in Russia. The contrast between Stalin and Khrushchev was itself amazing. Khrushchev was a long step up in leadership quality. Now Gorbachev has gone beyond Khrushchev and exhibits qualities of leadership that are quite unusual. With the counsel and support of advisers including Politburo member Alexander Yakovlev, who was a Fulbright scholar at Columbia University in 1958, and of former ambassador Anatoly Dobrynin, both of whom had acquired extensive first-hand knowledge of the United States, Gorbachev has demonstrated both imagination and a highly developed sensitivity to world conditions, as well as considerable courage in his apparent willingness to change the old order. Fortunately, Reagan, although quite unresponsive throughout most of his presidency, improved notably at the end, and now President Bush, if able and so inclined, has the opportunity to work with Gorbachev toward achievements of potentially historical consequence.

We do not have to approve of the social and political system of the Soviet Union, but it is unrealistic and a mistake not to accept its status as a great power. It is an illusion to believe that we can ever intimidate the Russians by military superiority any more than they can intimidate us, and equally an illusion to believe that we can force them into bankruptcy by outspending them for military weapons. The plain fact is that there is no reasonable prospect that we can eliminate or neutralize the other superpower's ability to injure us with nuclear weapons; but there is at least a possibility that we can, by persistent and carefully designed programs of confidence-building joint ventures, persuade them as well as ourselves of the advantages of more cooperative relations between us. By maintaining parity of military power at a lower level than at present, we can engage in cooperative joint ventures with little or no risk to our security.

Powerful though they are, the Soviet Union and the United States are under certain constraints that do not necessarily apply to other nations. The superpowers alone have the power—and with it the responsibility—to maintain a semblance of order in our turbulent world. Many other nations, large and small, have acquired the means to fight wars, trouble their neighbors, and disrupt their regions, if they are so inclined. In this respect we live in an increasingly pluralistic world. But in another, perhaps more important, respect, the paramount role of the superpowers is increasing rather than decreasing. They alone have the power, through collaboration, to put limits on the world's turbulence, to prevent great conflicts and contain small ones, to curb the excesses of nationalism and ambition, including their own, and by so doing to make the world as safe as it can be made in the thermonuclear age. Because of their power, and the responsibility it confers, the superpowers do not have the freedom to quarrel that smaller and less potentially dangerous nations have, or that great powers themselves had in an age when weapons were less destructive. The superpowers are therefore under an obligation—to themselves, to the rest of the world, and to posterity—to resolve their differences insofar as they can, and to set aside those that they cannot resolve. As the greatest threats to world peace, the United States and the Soviet Union also have the greatest responsibility for protecting it. That is the real meaning of détente. It is not, fundamentally, an option, but a compelling obligation.

2

Our Constitutional and Political Impasse

Our constitutional system, based on the principle of separation of legislative and executive powers, is showing serious weaknesses. The national elections for president have become superficial television extravaganzas producing candidates with little experience in foreign affairs. In many ways the parliamentary system is a superior form of democracy. It does not have our separation between the executive and the legislature, which obstructs accountability for governmental policies and actions and promotes the spread of adversarial conflict throughout the political process. Ours is a unique system; we are the only major democracy that has it. It leads to indecision and stalemate. And it is growing inadequate for the formulation of a coherent, rational foreign policy.

As a senator, I did not dwell too much on the essential weaknesses of our constitutional system. It was and remains a taboo subject. If you question our particular form of democracy, people don't argue about the merits of the case; they attack you personally, making it politically damaging to an elected official to discuss such matters. I suggested while serving recently on a committee to consider our constitutional system that we consider modifying the separation-of-powers principle and move toward adapting some of the features of the parliamentary system. No one said that the proposal was without merit, or that the parliamentary system was inferior to our own. They simply said that the American people would not accept it. Period. They made it clear that there was no use suggesting, or even talking about, the possible adoption of a parliamentary form of government in America. I suggested that we consider putting a paragraph in the commission's report to the effect that the concept of the parliamentary system should be seriously studied. With the exception of a few members, they were no more willing to question the validity of the principle of separation of powers than to discuss the virginity of the Virgin Mary. We have come to regard our constitutional system as we regard the Bible. Like the Chinese emperor of old, our presidential office, if not the presidents themselves, is perceived as invested with the mandate of heaven. It is a matter of blind faith, not common sense.

Early in my political career some of my sentiments about parliamentary government caused me a great deal of trouble with President Truman. In 1946 I had been asked to make speeches on behalf of the Democratic Party in the congressional election that year, although Truman himself was not up for election until 1948. It was pretty clear that things were not going to go well for the Democrats.

The Friday before the election in November 1946 I came back from campaigning and was sitting in the cafeteria in the old Senate Office Building, and Scott Lucas from Illinois came in. We were having a cup of coffee and gossiping about the election, talking about what the prospects were for the Democrats retaining control of the Senate and of the House. It was obvious that there was going to be a considerable turnover. The war was over; Roosevelt was dead. We had just seen Churchill defeated in Great Britain after the war and Attlee take over. It was clear that something comparable was going to happen in the United States. So we were talking about this and several press people joined us. It wasn't a press conference, just a bull session. The press was not there to record anything or take notes; it was just an informal discussion.

There was a reporter there from UPI named Anne Hicks. In the course of our discussion it was more or less agreed that we would probably lose the House. They were all up for election. But in the Senate, since only a third were up, there would have to be a real groundswell to change control there. So we judged that we were likely to lose the House, but not the Senate.

Then the question was: What if we lose both? What if we lose control of the Senate? Wouldn't this be a bad situation, with a president who was not elected, who succeeded as a vice-president, and both houses led by the opposition party? Wouldn't it create a chaotic situation? We had seen some of the consequences of this division between the executive and the legislature on a partisan basis at perilous times before—in Woodrow Wilson's and in Herbert Hoover's last years in office. It had led to frustration, stagnation, and stalemate.

I volunteered that if this happened, and since there was no vice-president, it might be good for the country for Truman to designate whomever the Republican Party wished as secretary of state. Under the law at that time the secretary of state was next in line of succession to the presidency. Then Truman should resign. A Republican could then become president and would have the support of the majority of both houses. In my academic, speculative mind, this seemed logical at the time, and I held forth on it for a while, exhibiting that I was aware of what a parliamentary system was all about. I made what I thought was a good case. If Truman remained as president and the Congress was against him, he would have a difficult time running the government. Not only would he be discredited as a leader, but it would be very difficult for the country, as we were faced with the daunting tasks of shaping an entirely new foreign policy after the war and rebuilding our economy.

47

It never occurred to me at the time that I was treading in dangerous waters or even that my comments might come to the attention of President Truman.

I went back to my office. I had been in the Senate for less than two years. To my surprise I got a telephone call from Anne Hicks. She asked if she could come and see me. I was flattered. Newspaper reporters seldom wanted to see a freshman senator in those days. So I said, "Sure, come on over."

She came over and said she was very interested in what I was saying about what should happen if the Congress went Republican. She said that she had never thought about the issue quite as she had heard it discussed; she hadn't thought about what a parliamentary system was or how it worked. She said she understood this had been an informal discussion, but was it all right with me if she wrote about it?

I said, "No, I don't want you to write it." It had been assumed for the sake of the argument, in that conversation in the cafeteria, that the Democrats would lose the Senate, but in fact I didn't think we would lose the Senate. This was just speculation as to the nature of our government, about a theory of government, and I had made the point that in the long run we should consider moving in the direction of a parliamentary system as more efficient and more democratic.

And she said, "Well, supposing it does happen that in the election the Democrats lose both houses, then do you mind if I use it?"

"If it happens, and I don't think it will," I said, "then I think it might be all right, because I think these are issues that the American people ought to know about and consider."

As it turned out, we lost both houses of Congress. I had gone with my wife, Betty, to stay with her family in Philadelphia over the weekend to await the election. I was awakened early in the morning the day after the election by a reporter.

"What is this story in the morning paper that you said Truman should resign?" he asked.

Obviously, I was in deep trouble. When I returned to Washington I prepared a thorough explanation for my suggestion, making the case that this could be good for the country and the Democratic Party, that the times were too perilous for this nation to bicker and drift for two years without a unified, responsible government. Nor was there much doubt as to the opinion of the people regarding the present administration, I said.

A few newspapers, like the *Chicago Sun,* endorsed the idea. Most of them took it as the idea of a young upstart who didn't understand our system and how wonderful it is.

I'm afraid Truman took it personally. I hadn't thought of it this way at all. When a reporter asked Truman, he said—off the record, I assume—that I was an overeducated SOB who should have gone to an American land-grant college instead of Oxford—or words to that effect. Relations with Mr. Truman were never very good after that. I was made to feel ridiculous; clearly I had violated a taboo of American politics.

I regret what happened to my relations with Truman. I rarely was invited thereafter to participate in any meeting with him, and it was no small political problem for me. Fortunately—at least from my point of view—for other reasons, Truman lost much of his popularity in the country and it wasn't held against me in my election in 1950. So I survived.

Years later Truman wrote me that he had been misquoted. "I made the remark that if you had attended a land-grant college in the United States instead of Oxford, you would never have made that statement. I never made any reflection on your personal character nor on your mother." Now Truman was being gracious, so I refrained from answering that I *had* attended a land-grant college. In July 1954—to even things out—I suggested that Eisenhower resign if the Democrats won control of the Congress. We did, but my comments then were largely ignored.

And yet, in history, what actually happened after 1946? In the 1948 election, Truman ran denouncing the no-good, no-account Eightieth Congress. Virtually everything that I said was likely to happen did happen, except that Truman wasn't discredited. But the election of 1948 was something of a miracle; everyone had thought he would lose. Yet even his victory doesn't change what I was trying to get at. Was the country better off with Truman elected? I think not. This fifth successive presidential defeat so frustrated the Republicans that it fed directly into the McCarthy period. It created a kind of bitterness in our political system, a meanness, that I think accounts for much of what was to come with Joseph McCarthy. Those years were disastrous ones for us; the atmosphere engendered by the Republicans' defeat, and by their irresponsibility, aggravated the cold war and contributed to that animosity toward the Russians that plagues us to this day.

The surprise Democratic victory of 1948 so embittered the Republicans that they seized upon the threat of communism with uncommon ferocity. It affected some of the most decent Republicans. Senator Robert Taft of Ohio was one of those. He didn't have anything in common with McCarthy. He was anything but a demagogue. But the election of Truman in '48 created such animus in him that he became desperate, willing to do anything to discredit the Democrats. He was a prominent and reputable member of the elite, the son of a president and chief justice, and had become a leading senator with plausible presidential ambitions of his own. He felt entitled to be important. And the bitterness of defeat was such as to make him support McCarthy. I liked him and played golf with him. He was a very hardworking, conscientious public servant; it was an aberration for him to support McCarthy. But he thought McCarthy was discrediting those dreadful Democrats. And so he went along. The partisan bitterness of those years was damaging to the country. It did succeed also in discrediting the Democrats.

We have not completely recovered yet. You see the periodic revival of the same kind of sentiment, this paranoiac anticommunism. Reagan's initial rhetoric was a virulent revival of the old McCarthy attitude that proved successful, politically, in so many cases. It has been the Republican Party's most reliable issue and avenue to power in the postwar era.

People often ask me why I voted against McCarthy—why I cast the single vote in the Senate in 1954 against funding Senator McCarthy's witchhunting subcommittee. I can only say that his manner and his methods were offensive to me. I thought him to be a demagogue and a ruthless boor.

They used to have an old saying down home: "You don't engage in a pissing contest with a skunk." People who were real stinkers, you left alone. Even though you didn't like them, you didn't bother with them, because they could do to you what a skunk could do—and you couldn't get rid of it, no matter what you said and did. It's a very earthy and sensible attitude. And most people are wise enough not to challenge it.

I tried not to get involved, but it was too much for me. I didn't like McCarthy from the time I became aware of him. We used to pass in the corridors, but we ignored each other. We had no personal conversations. Almost from the beginning I found I could not avoid a contest with this skunk.

I first became aware of him in the Banking and Currency Committee. There was a new project of prefabricated homes being carried out by the Lustron Company that had been financed by the Reconstruction Finance Corporation (RFC). The company failed, with considerable loss to the RFC. It turned out that McCarthy, while on the committee, had accepted a $10,000 fee to write something for the company, to promote it. That first made me aware of him, and suggested too that he was insensitive to a conflict of interest. We couldn't do much about this obvious conflict, as there was no Ethics Committee at the time. The incident, though, indicated what he was like, and called for some criticism from the rest of us, which I'm sure he didn't like.

My next encounter with McCarthy came when Senator Tom Connally, then chairman of the Foreign Relations Committee, appointed Senators John Sparkman and Guy Gillette, and me, as a subcommittee to hear witnesses on the nomination of Phillip Jessup to be a judge on the International Court. McCarthy attacked Jessup as being soft on communism. This was the beginning of his general attack upon people in public life, which later spread to teachers, the army—practically anybody if he thought the attack would draw attention to his hearings. He came to the hearings on Jessup with some documents that he had put on pink paper. His sense of showmanship inspired him to put on pink paper his allegations regarding Jessup's activities, including such transgressions as Jessup's membership in an organization called the Institute of Public Relations. Jessup was unreliable, in McCarthy's eyes; he wasn't a loyal American.

I was deeply offended by McCarthy's presentation and tactics. It was such obvious demagoguery. We had some very hard exchanges. I thought he was disgusting and irresponsible, trying to prejudice people by appealing to their worst instincts. We had quite an exchange of words.

People were beginning to be afraid of McCarthy; his allegations left people embarrassed and humilated. It didn't matter what the facts were. He destroyed the reputations of people and made them feel destroyed, even though there was little or nothing to his allegations. The publicity was enough to destroy many of them. People in public life were very sensitive to the effect that his allegations would leave on the public mind. And it got worse and worse.

Then in early 1954 there came to the Senate floor a bill for appropriations for McCarthy's subcommittee. I simply thought he was a scoundrel and voted no, and much to my surprise I was the only one who voted no. I thought that other people had sensed that this fellow was no good. But they all voted for it.

Enormous publicity resulted from that vote. I received between ten and twenty thousand cards and letters within a short period—insulting, degrading, vulgar communications that said I was a communist a "commy symp," or a dupe.

Subsequently Ralph Flanders, a Republican from Vermont, made some critical comments about McCarthy on the Senate floor. And there were a few others. I got the idea then of exploring the possibility of a censure resolution, because he was becoming a serious menace to the country. So I drew up a censure motion. I researched it. It had been years since there had been such a motion in the Senate. A few had been introduced back at the turn of the century, but those had had to do with physical fighting on the floor of the Senate. There was one case involving a Senator Bingham from Connecticut about 1929 that served as an example.

I took my proposal to Senator Carl Hayden of Arizona and Senator Walter George of Georgia, then the senior members of the Senate. I asked what they thought of it. "This fellow is just getting out of hand," I said. I knew they disapproved of him. But they were reluctant to become identified with public criticism of McCarthy. To be identified in the public press as quarreling with him was risky. But I found him so distasteful that I went ahead.

My distaste was heightened by the fact that, in an appropriations committee hearing, he had criticized the Fulbright educational exchange program. He said in effect that some of the participating scholars were subversive and that the people we were bringing into the country from Russia were KGB agents. That simply infuriated me. Again we had a very blunt exchange.

The senators to whom I took the censure resolution agreed that it was justified, but they didn't want to engage in a direct confrontation with McCarthy. But they didn't discourage me. They approved the idea of censure, so I went to Flanders. The reason I didn't put the resoultion in myself was that I knew that if I did—being a Democrat, and already having had a fight with McCarthy—it would immediately inspire partisanship. There would be Republicans who didn't know too much about the issues thinking that here was an attempt by the Democrats to embarrass them. Flanders was a respected and senior Republican.

I asked Flanders if he would introduce the resolution; I would cosponsor it. And I would do everything I could to help it pass. But his introduction would keep it from being a partisan measure. He agreed, and after the introduction the leadership appointed a special committee to consider the censure motion, headed by Senator Arthur Watkins of Utah, a conservative Republican. In the end, a great majority of the Democrats and about half of the Republicans voted to censure. And that was the beginning of the end of McCarthy.

But it was not the end of McCarthyism. His impact was disastrous. It did me great political harm in the long run, and especially during the years of my opposition to the Vietnam War, because this McCarthy business was in the back of people's minds. There was a kind of aura about me that "he's not really a good, one-hundred-percent American." I lost the support of people like George Meany of the AFL-CIO and the leaders of the American Legion. Throughout the rest of my career, this undercurrent remained. I could never completely get rid of it. The smell of the skunk remained.

The vote against McCarthy confirmed in the minds of many people the idea that I didn't understand that communism was a serious threat, a dangerous movement, and that I was rather a country bumpkin from Arkansas who didn't know anything about the real, vicious world in which we lived. Very few people called me a communist—although McCarthy himself, as I recall, said I was a communist sympathizer and called me "Half Bright."

For reasons including but by no means confined to the lingering impact of McCarthyism, our political system is functioning very poorly today. It is proving almost impossible either to seriously debate an important issue or to arrive at a consensus on how to handle it. But we have celebrated our system of checks and balances for so long that we now ignore the ways in which it weakens our government with a dynamic of adversarial relationships that frustrates any coherent policy. The executive frustrates Congress, one side checks another; and for much of the time—usually during Republican administrations—one party controls Congress, the other the executive.

The constitutionally built-in rivalry between executive and legislature is greatly aggravated when Democrats control Congress and there is a Republican president. The inevitable result is acute bickering, polemical stalemate, and governmental paralysis. Each side blames the other for our national failures. And the effects are by no means confined to domestic matters, because the world today has become so integrated that it is all but impossible to draw any line between foreign and domestic affairs.

Because of this intense competition, this adversarial relationship, neither party and neither branch of government has been willing to take the responsibility for advocating a major tax increase. With the exception of a few diehard supply-siders, everyone knows that we have been living since 1980 far beyond our means, that we are mortgaging our children's future; but for reasons largely (though not entirely) related to the nature of our political system, we find ourselves incapable of doing what we very well know we ought to do. Gramm-Rudman notwithstanding, Congress in recent years has often been unable to agree on a budget, much less a balanced budget, or to significantly reduce the deficit. Without wishing in any way to deny former president Reagan his full share of credit for this prodigal irresponsibility, I suggest that the perpetuation of the resulting situation and our inability to correct it is to a great extent due to the rivalry between executive and legislature that is inherent in our system of separation of the powers of government.

In these conditions it is very nearly impossible for us to reach any consensus on the issues we face today. Consider, by contrast, Japan. People always point to the homogeneity and the long cultural traditions of the Japanese as determinants of their considerable political harmony. But they also have a governmental mechanism to bring to bear on international relations that enables them to coordinate policies and reach consensus. They are not incessantly quarreling over every policy and contending for power and prestige within the government. At the risk of being elitist, I suggest that there is merit in the way the Japanese periodically change their leadership—quickly, quietly, and with little or no public discord. There is something commendable here.

Having exposed myself to the charge of elitism, I might as well continue. Originally, our system worked because it was built upon a close-knit elite, a distinct class, a small group of well-educated Anglo-Saxons who designed the Constitution.

They thought there would be such an elite, I suppose, for all time—a cosmopolitan, educated one much like themselves. They felt, as Madison expressed it in *Federalist* No. 10, that a governing elite of "fit characters" would have respect for the principles outlined in the Constitution, and that the members of this select group could be relied on to choose a competent chief executive from among their number. I think this is why, in those early days, despite reservations, the framers accepted the separation of powers. They assumed that we would indeed have "fit characters" running the country.

We should remember that Madison's original Virginia plan, submitted at the beginning of the convention in 1787, provided for the selection of the president by Congress. There was no practical historical precedent for the principle of separation of powers; only the ideas of such theorists as Montesquieu supported such a concept.

With the passage of time we have become a heterogeneous body of people derived from many countries and cultures, and while it cannot be said that we lack a common culture, our American culture, with preeminence given to the rights of the individual, does not foster political cohesion. The separation of powers, together with the diversity of our people, creates formidable obstacles to orderly government. Further, with the decline of the influence of traditional political parties, and with the great costs of television fostering the growth of private interest groups—or "political action committees," as they are called—to meet those costs, the powers of the federal government have become fragmented and dissipated, making it all too easy for organized private bodies to work their will on the government. In practice the separation of powers does not protect the interests of the community or of the individual citizen; on the contrary, it subjects them to exploitation by the special interests.

With the decline of the parties there is little sense of continuity in leadership, and we end up with a government of amateurs. It is almost impossible to develop a sense of the national interest or a foreign policy rooted in the national interest. And the very serious result is that no one is clearly and positively accountable. The public is confused and unable to tell who is responsible for our difficulties, so they end up thinking all politicians are bad and that government as such is bad and should be reduced and restrained. Rather than concentrating our efforts to make government better, we restrict it and condemn it, as President Reagan did when he said government was not the solution to our problems, that it was the problem.

Despite the enormous growth of presidential power, the capacity of American presidents to represent our country effectively in relations with other nations is seriously flawed. This circumstance is not an accident. It is the direct outgrowth of the determination of the Founding Fathers to prevent another tyranny such as occurred under George III. With good reason they were fearful of the power of the old monarchs. That, however, is not our problem now. What we need today is someone who can speak for the country.

That is not what we have. Even before Reagan's popularity began to decline with the Iran-contra scandal, there was always a question whether any agreement he signed would be approved by a Democratic Congress. Presidential agreements are inevitably tentative and provisional. Nixon's agreements with the Russians were effectively undercut in Congress. Foreign leaders, for their part, hesitate to make agreements with a leader who cannot deliver. They may commit themselves to a course of action that fails, and then they look like failures.

It stands to reason that if you are going to make a deal with somebody, you want it to be definite. When the prime minister of a parliamentary democracy signs on the dotted line, you can be sure, in most instances, that the agreement is going to be approved. You cannot be sure under our system. It is a complicated question, but many, usually adverse consequences follow from our inability to act coherently as a nation. The ultimate consequence is the casting into doubt of our reliability and with it of our ability to prevent a nuclear war and the development of conflict between nations. How, then, are we to speak clearly with other countries, particularly with the Soviet Union? How do we get a leader who can speak authoritatively for our country and articulate a viable foreign policy?

This is not to devalue the importance of debate. I participated in more than a few debates during my thirty years in the Senate, and I did not take kindly to suggestions that I ought to have remained silent. The stifling of democratic debate is not, however, a requisite for authoritative executive leadership. We need debate—but we also need the means of bringing debate to an end, of reaching a decision and standing by it. What presidents dislike about Congress, I suspect, is not debate but the inability to end it and reach a solid decision. That is what drives them to ignore and circumvent Congress—even, as in the cases of Watergate and Iran-contra, to the point of deception and illegality. This is also what drives presidents into the isolation and arbitrariness of what has come to be called the imperial presidency. We thus end up with the worst of two worlds: an isolated and arbitrary presidency and a quarrelsome, irrelevant Congress.

Perhaps the greatest difference between a president and a prime minister is that a prime minister in a parliamentary system must meet his peers and critics face to face; he must respond to criticisms, answer questions, endure the barbs and insults of the opposition. His presence in the House is not a state occasion filled with the trappings of ceremony and pomp associated with a president's visit to Congress. It is this power of parliament to continually require the prime minister to explain and justify his policies to an informed body of colleagues that is crucial.

It is not *confidence* in the technical sense that a prime minister must retain, but confidence in the ordinary sense—confidence in his competence, ability, and judgment.

The reciprocal requirement is *respect* for the legislature by the executive. If the president and his assistants lack respect for Congress, if indeed they are contemptuous of Congress as recent presidents and some of their influential advisers were, they can at least temporarily ignore or circumvent the House and Senate, and as a practical matter Congress can't do much about it. The particular issue is not usually serious enough to provoke an impeachment; and Congress's protest just makes it look all the more ineffective. There is no process such as a parliamentary vote of no confidence, a relatively easy way to show disagreement with the executive. That is the essence of our constitutional impasse: the legislature often lacks confidence in the executive, and the executive lacks respect for the legislature, and neither one, ultimately, can do very much about it.

It is not just a question of the past few presidents lacking experience, as Carter and Reagan certainly did. The adversarial relationship is built into our system. The incoherence in our policy, our inability to face our problems, is a failure not just of individual leaders, but of the system itself. It's not working; and as our problems mount, the dangers that come from this are rapidly escalating.

With all our much-praised checks and balances, we cannot confront a president head on. No president ever has to explain his views in detail, or reconcile them with criticisms or suggestions made by others. Few journalists, however tough-minded, wish to give offense to a president; nor do they have the special interest that a leader of the political opposition does in exposing misjudgments and mistakes.

The president today practically lives and acts like a king. Although a mighty propaganda machine strives ceaselessly to convince us otherwise, he is not just one of the boys. He is not first among equals. When you surround a person with such adulation and security, he starts to lose all sense of reality. There is no one, as George Reedy wrote, to tell him to go soak his head. It was bad enough with Lyndon Johnson, but it has been worse since. Johnson had had a lot of experience with Congress; he didn't feel the contempt for it that a man who has never been in it feels. Now we have presidents acting in ways that suggest they feel quite superior to Congress; Reagan seemed to feel that he didn't even belong to the government. He stood aside from it; government, as he often said, was the problem, not the solution, and not something he was a part of. He was above it. You see presidents, for their own purposes, cultivating a contempt for Congress on the part of the people. They encourage the popular perception of Congress as mean-spirited and corrupt, which is reflected in the low approval rating for Congress so often expressed in the polls. The president evades responsibility for the ills of the nation by denigrating Congress.

In a parliamentary system, the people who select the chief executive have often worked with him or her for twenty years or longer. Most prime ministers have had years of experience in parliament before becoming the leader of the government. To a considerable degree, the basis for their selection is the way they have performed their duties as members of parliament over that period. And those who choose them are those who work with them. They are selected by peer review, in marked contrast to our popular elections, where ninety-five percent of the people who select our leaders have only seen them on television. You don't know them at all other than how they appear, how their images are shaped, how entertaining they are, how conciliatory their manner. Do they have ingratiating smiles, nice eyes, pretty teeth, plenty of hair? Look at Reagan's hair, for example, done up every day to look perfect, without a gray strand. This is not to criticize the former president—I may even be a bit envious. My criticism is directed at the superficiality of political media marketing and its utter irrelevance to competent leadership. But marketing, it seems, is the name of the game. Appearance and manner, not intellect or character, are the commodities required for the selling of the president, and it's all made up, part of the act. This is not to suggest that we never get a president with intellect and character, only that when we do, it is something of an accident.

There are good reasons why the Founding Fathers were dubious about the direct election of the president. Madison's plan would have had Congress elect the president, but the idea got lost in a compromise on the electoral college. There was almost no support among the framers for popular election of the president. A further, more informal method of peer review in the early years of the Republic was the selection of presidential candidates by the party caucuses in Congress, and by and large they came up with qualified candidates.

There are lots of people—and lots of special interests—in this country who do not want our government to be more decisive and united. They like it as it is, because the multiple points of access available to "political action committees" and other lobbying groups make it much easier for these special interests—ranging from ethnic lobbies to Pentagon contractors—to get what they want, and they have become a major influence on our government. The public interest gets lost in the rivalry between these private interests. A parliamentary system does not necessarily eliminate the special interests, but I do think it minimizes their power and impact. One major advantage is that elections are not strictly national but by districts. Were we to divide the United States into 535 districts—the total number of representatives and senators—each constituency would be in the neighborhood of 500,000, a not unmanageable size. It is not beyond the capacity of a candidate to be personally acquainted with many of the constituents. Candidates—and constituents—would not have to rely primarily on thirty-second spots on television. I don't know how you get rid of the abuses injected by television, but I do think they could be minimized, ameliorated to a degree, with elections at the district level.

In this highly democratic fashion we could choose a representative Congress or "parliament," from whose number a president or "prime minister" would then be chosen in precisely the same manner that the presidents of well-run corporations or universities are usually chosen—by peer review. Who indeed is likely to have a better judgment of the best candidate—those working with a potential leader for twenty years through parliamentary procedure, or the mass of voters forced to choose from the slickly packaged political products they see on television? Our present system *can* produce capable leaders, but a felicitous result, when it occurs, is essentially accidental.

The way our system is structured, it is exceedingly difficult to move through the congressional system up to the presidency, to gain the approval of your peers in ways that allow for choice of leadership. Howard Baker is a good example. He was a leader of the Senate, but he thought it necessary to resign to run for the presidency—a purpose from which he was subsequently sidetracked. Had he been his party's leader in a parliamentary system, I expect he would have become the prime minister. Similarly, it always seemed to me during my own years in the Senate that the highly respected Richard Russell of Georgia would inevitably have become a prime minister, but Russell, as a southerner with an anti-civil-rights voting record, was never a credible candidate for president.

A parliament would not have chosen Reagan or Carter, for the same reason that a major university or corporation would not have hired a movie actor or an obscure former governor as president: they lacked relevant credentials. With the Carter and Reagan administrations, we had two presidents who had no previous experience in the federal government. Both surrounded themselves in the White House, and to some degree too in their cabinets, with old friends and cronies, who also had no experience in the government. When it comes to appointments, they did not personally know many of the people who had been prominent, active, and effective in the political system of the national government. They had to rely on the advice of professionals they had only recently met, and in other cases they simply picked rank amateurs.

Carter simply couldn't cope with the bureaucracy and the Congress. The people he brought with him were quite well-intentioned, fine young men. But they had no experience and did not know how to operate. They did not have any of those long-established personal relationships that experienced professionals have. Government, like everything else, is dependent on these relationships, and on the personal trust associated with them, which can hardly be developed with a new crowd of people coming in every four years, eager to change previous policies. You can't bring in a whole new crowd every four or even eight years who want to change previous policies and learn on the job. It does not work very well, as the last two administrations richly demonstrated.

The Iran-contra affair shows what happens when you put people in with no experience in the operations of government, no familiarity with its procedures, and indeed with no apparent credentials except energy and zealotry. They are not conscious of any restraints; they don't have any feeling—or apparently much concern—as to whether their actions are in accord with the Constitution or the law. They act like rogue elephants, or perhaps more like children with a new toy. They go off and do whatever they want, all the more eagerly when the president gives evidence of being indifferent and uninformed. They are not conscious of any of the restrictions that you get from association. If you have experience with people who are acquainted with proper legal and constitutional procedures, and accustomed to complying with them, you are influenced by them. If you don't have that kind of influence, you tend to do just what comes to you naturally, without guidance or prudential restraint.

Carter didn't consult with many of the most experienced Washington people. I don't think he consulted Clark Clifford, for example, although Clifford had something that Carter sorely lacked but seemed not to know he needed: the judgment that comes with experience. Clifford had been in and out of government since Truman's day, when he had been the president's speechwriter and confidant. But Carter made no attempt to draw on that kind of experience.

I would add, at the risk of being personal, that he never consulted me either. That caused me no distress—except with respect to the Fulbright educational exchange program, with which I had been associated for over thirty years. Without consulting me, or giving me advance notice, he transferred the administration of the program from the State Department to the U.S. Information Agency. I couldn't stop it and I still feel it was a great mistake. Carter, I think, didn't know anything about it; he only had some theoretical idea of simplifying the bureaucracy. It wasn't that he had anything against the program. It was just a lack of knowledge about its history and purpose, and perhaps he didn't think it was important anyway.

Another great weakness of our system is how hard it is to get rid of an inadequate leader. In a parliamentary system, if you have a serious problem with an issue of judgment, it is not such an extraordinary thing. Leaders who for one reason or another have become an embarrassment can be removed by a vote of no confidence, or more commonly, by a quietly arranged resignation. When Britain's Middle East policy collapsed at the time of Suez in 1956, Anthony Eden was out in two weeks, embarrassed but not disgraced, and the country was enabled to proceed with the conduct of its business. We cannot do that. Not only do our elections go on for two years; our scandals last almost as long. It is senseless and debilitating. Watergate distracted us for two years. In a parliamentary system Nixon would have been forced to resign early on and perhaps been packed off to the House of Lords.

In addition, there is very little sense of continuity in our political system any longer. It has been undermined throughout the government. There used to be some continuity in the Senate, but even there it is declining, as senators serve for shorter periods, in a number of instances leaving voluntarily. There is indeed a large turnover; the number of senators retiring who are not doing so because of age is quite unusual. There used to be an organized hierarchy in Congress that made the legislative machinery operate with some efficiency. That too is breaking down, with the dismantling of the seniority system and the weakening of party leadership.

When I arrived in the Senate in 1945, the seniority system was still strong. Precedence and position were governed by the principle of seniority, which, though not wholly democratic, had the advantage of being automatic, and the greater advantage of giving weight to experience. Although I sometimes chafed under it, I made no serious objection. We used to joke about it sometimes, that the old boys were imposing on us. But I abided by it and I never tried to challenge it. In time I came to appreciate that it was a sound method of restraining the development of internal rivalry and bitterness. It provided housekeeping rules and thus removed the management of the Congress from political conflict.

Television has contributed to the Senate's transformation. Even the televising of the hearings tends to create a very different atmosphere and very different type of debate. If you talk too long and give too much substance regarding your positions, they'll turn you off. You've got to make it lively. The trouble is that serious issues are not always all that lively, to say nothing of entertaining. A real debate about the state of our relations with the Russians, for example, might be boring at times. It would quite properly touch on a fair amount of the history and the actions of these two nations over a long period of time—and that sort of discussion does not make for good television entertainment.

In the old days, the debates were in fact interesting and often, to the members, quite enjoyable. Many of us found it extremely interesting to debate serious issues on the Senate floor. The ABM treaty in 1972 generated a real debate, as did the first SALT agreement. I hesitate to point back to the great debates over such programs as the Marshall Plan in the 1940s involving senators like Richard Russell, Walter George, Bob Taft, and Arthur Vandenberg. You are likely to be considered something of an old fogy when you harp on "the old days," but I simply fail to find any debate comparable in recent years. The debates over the sale of F-15s to Saudi Arabia in 1978 or of the AWACs in 1981 were not really significant debates as such. They were just debating arms sales, not the question of our policy toward Israel and the Middle East—except for a certain amount of rhetorical sentimentalizing. They were not examining what we could do to bring about a cessation of the threats of war in that area. All this has worked to lessen control over the chief executive, without leading to coherent criticism of policies and the formulation of coherent alternatives.

Another significant dilemma, from a senator's standpoint, is that in our system, unlike a parliamentary system, you have to give up your position in the Senate if you join the cabinet or become a presidential adviser. Then, if you have a difference with the president, you have to resign or he fires you. And you are out—out of the government. If we had had a parliamentary system, and I could have retained my seat in the Senate, I might well have accepted appointment as secretary of state if it had been offered—or at least would have been interested in it.

In any case, I was not offered the position of secretary of state by Kennedy. I was quite aware of the rumors at the time that I might be. Vice-president-elect Johnson evidently had recommended me to Kennedy. So I went to Dick Russell, who was very close to Johnson and also on good terms with Kennedy, and who was certainly the most influential Democratic senator at that time. I told Russell that I was not temperamentally suited to be secretary of state—a viewpoint in which my wife, Betty, wholeheartedly concurred. I had had a brief experience with State Department procedures as a delegate to the United Nations and had observed the workings of the State Department in the course of my duties on the Foreign Relations Committee. I didn't feel I was suited to be on a team and not have freedom of action to do or say whatever I thought about policies. For these reasons I told Russell he ought to tell the president-elect that it would be a mistake to name me as secretary of state. I preferred to stay where I was, where I thought I was best suited.

Russell said he would speak to Kennedy about it. I'm quite sure my judgment was correct. I don't think I would have been a successful secretary of state. I couldn't have administered somebody else's policy—or one I disagreed with.

Of course, I don't know if Kennedy was ever serious. He called me up after he appointed Dean Rusk and invited me to come visit him in Palm Beach, where he was visiting his father. He met me at the airport and took me to his father's home. He said he was sorry that there had been so much publicity about the matter and hoped it had not caused me any embarrassment. I told him not to be sorry at all, that I thought he'd done the right thing. At that time, I didn't know much about Rusk. Kennedy didn't either, in my opinion. I think he had just met him.

Joe Kennedy was very cordial when I had breakfast with him the next morning. He said Jack had been very interested in my being secretary of state, but that there were political difficulties with regard to the racial issue—that I had voted against the civil-rights acts, which was true, back in the forties and fifties, and that George Meany and the AFL-CIO were not sympathetic to my appointment. He also said that the Israeli representatives thought I was not sufficiently sympathetic to Israel, and that, all together, these were very important political considerations. A recent publication of the late Robert Kennedy's views contain a passage in which he takes credit for preventing my appointment.

I didn't feel that if I had been offered the job I could have turned it down. That is the reason I went to Russell. It would have been embarrassing to decline appointment as secretary of state. I thought it better to try to prevent that eventuality. If Kennedy had asked, I would probably have accepted and I strongly suspect that I would have quickly been out. I would have been out of the Senate too; and even if I could have returned, my seniority would have been lost. That is part of our system, and one that I think undercuts continuity of experience as well as the presence of critical, questioning voices who disagree with policy. It encourages people to remain in the government, to go along even when they disagree—or to simply break away but be ineffective. It doesn't work well, especially in foreign policy.

After three decades in public life, I am unable to generate enthusiasm or even sympathy for either a "strong" presidency or an assertive legislature as such. Within our current system, the best we can perhaps hope for is a shifting of emphasis according to the needs of the time and the requirements of public policy.

Among my many speeches on foreign policy over the years, only one that I gave at Cornell in May 1961 elicited much enthusiasm from the executive branch. I asked then if the time had not come when we were going to have to give the executive a greater measure of power to conduct foreign relations than had hitherto been the case.

In the aftermath of the relatively quiet Eisenhower years, I saw some merit in a more assertive exercise of executive power. I opposed the growing power of foreign lobbies over the Congress. Congressmen were sponsoring various pet projects quite inimical to shaping a coherent foreign policy. Individual senators were supporting specific projects in the annual aid bill that I thought distorted its original purpose. Previously the specifics of amount and conditions of aid had been left to the discretion of the executive. Now Congress began to interfere with that. I thought the executive needed greater authority to deal with such issues.

In later years, Dean Rusk—in hearings before the Foreign Relations Committee on the conduct of the Vietnam War, the Dominican intervention, and the national-commitments resolution—took considerable satisfaction in quoting my thesis of 1961 and commending it to the committee.

But after Eisenhower, a far more assertive view of presidential action prevailed. In the three succeeding presidencies—of Kennedy, Johnson, and Nixon—there was a dramatic resurgence of executive power. The armed forces were committed in Cuba in 1961 and the Dominican Republic in 1965—precipitately, without congressional sanction, and in violation of our inter-American treaty obligations. In Vietnam we fought a long, costly, futile war with no more cover of constitutional sanction than the dubious and later discredited Gulf of Tonkin resolution.

The reaction to the "imperial presidency" was an effort by many of us in Congress to reconsider the proper balance between Congress and the president in the making of foreign policy. The results include the national-commitments resolution of 1969, the Case Act of 1972 requiring the reporting of executive agreements, the war-powers resolution of 1973, and a whole series of legislative amendments restricting and finally ending American military action in Indochina.

Yet such arrangements, important as they are, probably cannot cope with the real problems, given our current constitutional system. I thought the war-powers resolution was a good idea, for example, although I was not a sponsor of it and I did not think it would be very effective. The problem is that such legislation depends for its effectiveness upon the president, and the executive, having respect for the Congress. If they have none, if the president is contemptuous of the Congress, as Nixon and Reagan were, and ignores it, then as a practical matter there is not too much that can be done. The specific instances of abuse of power are not usually serious enough to provoke impeachment. Laws like the war-powers resolution are not self-enforcing. If you don't have a way of making a vote of no confidence, if you lack a relatively easy way to show your disagreement with the executive, such legislation is not a very effective mechanism. The problems connected with the constitutional war powers of Congress in general and the war-powers resolution in particular are those that are built into the separation of powers. When the law is defied, as it has been, the Congress is then faced with the challenge of invoking the considerable authority at its disposal, but the members are usually too timid to consider that. If they really wanted to act, they would use the power of appropriations rather than, or in addition to, invoking the war-powers resolution. They might get farther, but they are usually too timid for that too.

The trouble with the resurgent legislature of the late 1970s is that it went in the wrong directions too often, carping and meddling, in the service of special interests, not engaging in reflective deliberation on basic issues of national interest. This tendency, once again, is tied to the general weakening of the party and leadership system in the Congress, which in turn has made Congress more susceptible to the pressures of special interests than previously. The executive thus with some justification complains about congressional incursions on its flexibility and its ability to make important decisions, or about Congress locking it in with legislative prohibitions. What executive branch officials choose to ignore is that Congress has been driven to this from the years of ignored advice.

For all his personal geniality, President Reagan was basically contemptuous of Congress. His particular version of the imperial presidency amounted to a belief that he could do anything he liked as commander-in-chief and chief executive. The Reagan administration defied the war-powers resolution; violated the Boland amendment regarding aid to the contras; "reinterpreted" the ABM treaty to give it a whole new meaning; and preached a doctrine of presidential prerogative that amounted to a claim that he had the right to ignore virtually all restraints.

Even sending American warships into the Persian Gulf war zone did not result in any invocation of the war-powers resolution. The executive evidently feels demeaned by the very suggestion, as though the powers of the commander-in-chief would be undercut by even the appearance of cooperating with the Congress. This passing of the actual means to initiate war—as distinguished from the legal authority—from the hands of Congress to those of the executive is one of the most remarkable, and largely unnoticed and still unappreciated, transformations of our Constitution.

The change in our world position drastically altered our constitutional practices after 1945. Time after time—from the undeclared naval war in the Atlantic with Germany and Italy in 1941, to the Korean War, to the Vietnam War and the invasion of Cambodia—the executive has undertaken large-scale military operations without even informing, let alone gaining approval from, Congress.

I don't think that our checks and balances really can cope with such strains and challenges as well as a parliamentary system could. In the name of national security, presidents have felt free to act on their own in Lebanon in 1958, the Bay of Pigs in 1961, the Gulf of Tonkin in 1964, the Dominican invasion of 1965, the blockade of North Vietnamese ports in 1972, not to mention Grenada and the Persian Gulf. Not one of these instances even remotely resembled a clear and present danger to our national security.

On numerous occasions, the Senate Foreign Relations Committee was told, essentially, to mind our own business—which is to say, refrain from getting involved in foreign policy—because we did not have the detailed secret information on which delicate and clandestine policies are based. There is some truth in this contention. Congress can act effectively in foreign policy only if it has the facts. Without these, it can hardly make enlightened decisions or render sound advice. But it is largely the executive, with its phalanx of experts, that has withheld crucial information. Was it a vital secret that we were conducting a secret war in Laos, far away from the North Vietnamese infiltration routes along the Ho Chi Minh trail? And if so, a secret from whom? Surely not from the North Vietnamese.

I don't see how under our present system we can effectively control the CIA or regulate clandestine activities. The established oversight system is all but inoperative when you have a president like Reagan and a director like William Casey, who simply have no respect for Congress, and wish to subvert it. Congress can pass legislation denying aid to the Nicaraguan contras, but laws are of little avail when Reagan goes ahead and does it anyway. The Church committee of the late seventies did a commendable job of trying to institutionalize oversight of the CIA. But nothing in the Iran-contra affair suggests it was really effective. What's the cure? The easiest thing is to say, "Get a good president." But then, our system is not one that enables us to select the best possible president.

Our division of authority is based on the assumption that our elected leaders will respect the rights and roles of others in the system—in short, that they will uphold the Constitution. When they do not, when the president decides that he is going to do whatever he wants to do, the system begins to break down. When I went to law school many years ago, I do not remember any professor or teacher telling about the inherent presidential power to make war, or the inherent presidential power to do this and that. They talked not about inherent powers but about constitutional powers.

What powers does the Constitution give the president? The Constitution does not give him the authority to initiate war.

So long as the army will obey his commands, he has the raw *power* to make war, and presidents have repeatedly done that—but violation of the Constitution does not change the Constitution, and usurpation, no matter how frequently practiced, does not constitute valid legal precedent.

I recognize, of course, that the parliamentary system can be abused too. If you get an extremely powerful prime minister who dominates his colleagues, grave abuses happen. But I think this is much less likely in the parliamentary system, whereas in our system it is commonplace.

For years before the Church committee did its work, I tried to establish some oversight of the CIA. These efforts did not get anywhere. Mike Mansfield and I offered a resolution for the creation of a formal oversight committee. It was defeated. The military and the CIA together had control, for all practical purposes at that time, of legislation that affected them. You could not pass anything that would give greater supervision and control. They just stressed how any limitations would endanger our security and secrecy. The entire range of covert CIA operations thus developed largely apart from congressional auspices. I don't believe that is going to change until we find alternative ways of organizing the entire conduct of our foreign relations.

Much has changed in the way we select our political leaders since I entered politics in 1941. I am sure this passing of some of those old ways shapes my views in many diverse ways. There was no television when I first ran for office; radio was hardly a factor in my early campaigns.

Until the summer of 1941, when I was removed as president of the University of Arkansas, I had never participated directly or indirectly other than as a voter in any political campaigns.

Our local congressman, Clyde Ellis, with whom I had become acquainted when he was a student and took my class in constitutional law, came from a little village north of Fayetteville. I used to lecture in that class on the theme that our democratic system required that people with education and knowledge about government should go into politics. I had also lectured that there had been a tendency by our leading citizens to avoid politics because the rewards of business and the professions were so much greater. When Clyde came to tell me he was giving up his House seat to run for the Senate (a race which he ultimately lost), he reminded me of what I had said. He recommended that I run for his seat in the House of Representatives. I would never have thought of the idea if he hadn't.

I said I didn't know many people in the district and had never traveled throughout the region. It was a geographically large area, though thinly populated in the Ozark Mountains, and very rugged. Now there are beautiful roads, but at that time there were no modern roads at all. The rural roads were extremely rough and rocky. I had gone fishing in quite a few of those counties, but I really didn't know the people. I didn't have any acquaintances at all in the eastern end of the district.

Ellis said he knew these people well. They had supported him in the last election; he would give me a list of people to call on and I could see what their reactions were. He was going to announce for the Senate at the end of the week, so I got into the car with Betty and we drove over to one county after another. What you did in those days was to go to the county seat, to the courthouse, and look up the county judge, the county sheriff, the county collector, or any of the other people active in politics. I did that, and found the reaction favorable enough so that, come that Saturday, at the same time that Clyde announced for the Senate, I announced for the House.

I had a Model A Ford coupe, and Betty and I traveled through the district. I had a speaker on top of the car, and a microphone that we put in the trunk—the rumble seat, really—and we started out. If we found a gathering, any group of people, why, we would pull out the microphone and speak. Mostly, though, it was just going into stores and meeting people on the street in these little villages, or you would see somebody on his front porch and stop by and talk, introduce yourself—talk about farming, or anything that seemed appropriate.

Never having made a political speech before, I found the first few efforts excruciatingly painful. I have seldom experienced a greater feeling of abject despair and humiliation than the first time I spoke on the streetcorner of a small village, with a dozen or so listeners, who apparently were not listening. However, it's amazing how soon one becomes accustomed to the sound of one's own voice when forced to repeat a speech five or six times a day. And you get a pretty intimate sense of the views and concerns of your constituents in the process.

This went on from February to June 1942, when the Democratic primary was held. After the first few weeks, the size of the crowds started to grow; they seemed more responsive and interested. Usually at night on a Friday or Saturday, you might get a few hundred people in the county seat; in the smaller towns in daytime, still only a handful; and in the larger towns, in the last week of the campaign, fairly good-sized crowds. There was no television, and no radio. We published a small pamphlet called the *Victory News*. It was a small tabloid newspaper, containing recipes, farming news, and such—and in between, a few pieces about me, what I had done.

We won. My principal opponent was a friend of Governor Homer Adkins, Carl Greenhall. He was a member of the Supreme Court of Arkansas at the time. He seemed not to take my candidacy very seriously, and that may have helped me win. In the end, we estimated the cost of the campaign at about $10,000, all of which was raised by me, my wife, and my mother—the family. And that was that.

I had married Betty—Elizabeth Williams—ten years before, and despite the very different world she came from, she proved an adept campaigner in Arkansas.

Betty was from Philadelphia, and I am not sure her mother approved of me at first. She apparently didn't think it was appropriate for her daughter to be interested in a man from Arkansas. In fact, she wasn't quite sure where Arkansas was. She knew it was out west, where Indians lived, and it was dangerous. Betty had been raised in a very parochial manner in Philadelphia, where there was a rather closed society that didn't feel anybody else was quite good enough to associate with them. You might say that Betty blossomed, however, in the freedom she found in Arkansas, for she came to love doing things of which she had had no knowledge before. She had never lived on a farm, and when we went back to Arkansas, we lived in a modernized log house. Betty immediately took up raising chickens and cultivating a garden. We had a cow, and she made cottage cheese and butter. We raised pigs and cured hams. These were all things that were completely alien to Betty's upbringing and experience. Her reaction was one of great curiosity and enthusiasm.

Betty got along well with people. Many people told me that they really liked her better than they did me, because she was more sympathetic. I think that my success in being elected five times to the Senate was to a great extent due to her.

She was quite gregarious. She hardly ever got on an airplane without making friends with whoever sat next to her. She just *liked* it. She was curious about them. She would prefer to talk to whoever was there than to read. I had the terrible weakness of thinking that an airplane flight was a good opportunity to read a book, because I wouldn't be interrupted. I never did have quite the same curiosity about my seatmate that Betty did.

Soon after I went to Congress in 1943, I received a lot of favorable publicity for the passage of the Fulbright resolution pledging U.S. membership in a future United Nations. I was acutely conscious at that time that, although the war was terrible, the attention span of the public was short. As soon as the war was over, people would want to forget it and would not want to do anything about future wars. It seemed important to bring out the resolution while the war was going on so that the Congress would consider the idea of a postwar peacekeeping organization and vote for or against it under the impact of war.

When I first arrived in Washington, I was assigned to the House Committee on Foreign Affairs, largely because there was no competition for it. It was not a politically attractive committee to be on. The committees that were—and are— desirable to members are Appropriations, Ways and Means, Agriculture, Commerce, and perhaps a few others that are directly related to the interests of a member's constituents. Foreign Affairs was not in that category. Wilbur Mills, a colleague from Arkansas, told me we already had members on Ways and Means and Appropriations from Arkansas, but since I had been a Rhodes Scholar, maybe I would like Foreign Affairs.

Almost immediately, I became involved in the hearings on Lend-Lease. As I listened, I began to inquire what we were going to get out of the program. We would help our friends fight the war, but couldn't we get something more tangible and more permanent? Couldn't we get a commitment to try to do something to avoid the recurrence of such a dreadful war? Couldn't we get some commitment that might revive the idea of the League of Nations but make it more effective? Could we commit ourselves to join such an organization?

Then the resolution occurred to me. I showed it around to my colleagues, especially Jim Wadsworth and Charles Eaton, both senior Republicans on the Foreign Affairs Committee. They both encouraged me and advised me. They told me what to do and whom to see, all that sort of thing—how to go about it—which I did. I took it as a project, so to speak.

Then I submitted the draft resolution to the State Department. Sumner Welles was acting secretary of state at the time. He reviewed it and sent me a letter approving the resolution as consistent with the president's program. With such support, it was approved by the committee. Then it went to the floor, where Sam Rayburn, the Speaker, at the request of Jim Wadsworth, put the resolution off until the fall in order to give Wadsworth the opportunity to submit it to the Republican conference to be held soon thereafter at Mackinac Island. The result was that it passed in September by a vote of 360 to 29.

After the resolution passed with such an overwhelming majority, Tom Connally, chairman of the Foreign Relations Committee in the Senate, brought out the Connally resolution, which was very similar. He didn't take up my resolution. But that was typical of Tom. He thought it was presumptuous of me in the first place. A House member had no business intruding into the foreign-relations field. That was for the Senate, not the House—and especially not for an unknown freshmen congressman. Nevertheless, the resolution received a great deal of favorable publicity. There were cartoons and editorials all over the country, and it was very unusual for a freshman congressman to get such favorable publicity. I'm sure, in the way things operate in politics, it was partly responsible for the encouragement I received soon thereafter to run for the Senate.

The political leaders in Arkansas were looking for a candidate to run for governor to succeed the incumbent, Homer Adkins. I didn't want to be governor. I was already in the House and in Washington, and I didn't see the point. Besides I had never run statewide; I had run only in the third district, and I didn't think I was a very good prospect to be elected governor in any case.

They shifted from the question of governor, then, to who was going to be the candidate for the Senate. These were people who were in opposition to the Adkins regime, including a number of people I had known over the years. The favorable publicity from the Fulbright resolution, I'm sure, contributed to the idea that I might be a viable senatorial candidate in the 1944 race.

I don't believe I would have run for the Senate if Governor Adkins had not emerged as the principal candidate. He had fired me from the university in what I guess you would say was a very personal way. And I didn't like the idea of being a congressman in a state delegation with Adkins as a senator. I would rather go back home than be in a secondary position to him. I had no idea what he might have been interested in if he had gotten into the Senate, but I doubted it would include matters of national consequence. Perhaps that is unfair to him because I never really knew him personally. The only contact I had had with him was his firing me from the university.

The incumbent senator, Hattie Caraway, had succeeded her husband and was not in a strong position. Her former sponsor, Huey Long of Louisiana, had been assassinated. Then there was Colonel Barton, a very rich oilman, who entered the race at the last moment. That muddied the waters and made the contest much more difficult than it otherwise might have been. My race cost $46,000, and I think Colonel Barton spent $110,000. That was big money in those days, and the colonel was quite extravagant. He imported the Grand Ole Opry from Tennessee, and they played their popular country music in some of the small towns to attract big crowds for Barton. I happened to be in Texarkana on one occasion, and I heard that Colonel Barton was going to appear with the Grand Ole Opry over at Stamps, a town not far away. So I, all by myself, drove over and parked by the edge of the crowd to see what it was like, because I had never heard him speak. The Grand Ole Opry would play for about twenty minutes and then Barton would speak for ten or twenty minutes, and then they would play again. So that the crowd wouldn't leave. At that time they were the most popular music troupe in the country. Barton's speech didn't impress me very much. He was a very dignified gentleman—a fine-looking, tall man—but he wasn't particularly articulate. He read his speech and it didn't impress me. So I felt rather encouraged afterwards. I went on about my business, not making my presence known to anybody. I was just there to see what it was like.

I came in first in the primary, but short of a majority, which necessitated a run-off against Governor Adkins, who came in second. He was my real opponent. Just a few days before the run-off election, he attacked me, in the racist idiom of the day, as a "nigger-lover." He made accusations that were highly inflammatory in the South in the 1940s: that I was for bringing the black people into the Democratic primary, letting them vote, integrating the schools. His attacks made my people at campaign headquarters rather desperate about the racial issue. For my own part, coming from Washington County in northwest Arkansas, where there were almost no black people, I was not acutely conscious of questions of race. Less than 1 percent of the population of Washington County at that time was black, and there was no interest or concern in Fayetteville, as I recall, with questions of racial integration. I had no experience with the issue, and I don't think I inherited any particular feelings about it from my family.

The most populous part of the state, however, was the eastern delta country, where in some six counties the black population was more than fifty percent. That is where racial questions were an extremely emotional, delicate issue centered around fears of miscegenation. What Adkins was implying, of course, was that I didn't share the racial concerns of the people. He made a lot out of one vote that I had cast in the House of Representatives involving the salary of a black employee of the Treasury Department. He had the Arkansas State Police and Highway Department take a pamphlet he had prepared and distribute it all over the state. It was not in the newspapers; the publication was just distributed by hand all over the state a few days before the run-off primary. Adkins probably thought there was not much I could do about it.

On the weekend before the runoff election, I went down to Pine Bluff and spoke at the football field. I said I was against the participation of black people in the Democratic primary. That was that. The race finally finished and I won, though it was pretty close.

There has always been an idea in this country, under our democratic traditions, that the people are the voice of God and that their elected representatives ought to follow exactly what they think. Until recently this outlook was modified by the willingness and ability of at least a few politicians to try to lead public opinion. But something very basic has changed in our political process. Today our elected representatives, and the "communications" experts they employ, study and analyze public attitudes by sophisticated new polling techniques. But their purpose has little to do with leadership, still less with education in any area of our national life. Their purpose seems to consist largely in discovering what people want and feel and dislike, and then in associating themselves with those feelings. They seek to discover which issues can be safely emphasized and which are more prudently avoided. This is the opposite of leadership; it is followership, elevated to a science, for the purpose of self-advancement.

Even formal policy speeches are determined by the polls. The policy statements that emerge have little if anything to do with the national interest. They are rather an amalgam of the opinions and prejudices of people who may or may not know anything about the issue—dressed up, of course, in the pompous, sanctimonious, maudlin, or self-serving phraseology that so many modern politicians believe will appeal to the voters. There is nothing at all wrong with a legislator performing services for his constituents. That's part of his work. But with a few notable exceptions, our modern legislators have discarded the role of educator in the process of devoting themselves to servicing local interests. And these interests are not always their constituents' interests as a community but those of the best-organized, best-funded, and most politically active interest groups within each constituency.

A responsible approach requires that a legislator have a policy or program—some conception or idea—that he believes to be in the national interest as well as in the best interests of his constituency. Salesmanship and technique may then be employed to win its enactment. But we are witnessing a new breed of congressperson who seems more inclined to test the market first, to ascertain what is the current demand, and then to try to formulate a program to fit the market. The new politician is a product of the age of television, with its commanding emphasis on image to the neglect of substance.

Some senators send out questionnaires and conduct regular polls, asking their constituents questions about the current

issues of the day, especially the controversial ones. They carefully tabulate the responses and tend to follow what the majority indicates. Most of these people stay in office indefinitely.
They just put in their time in the Senate or House, but I don't
think they accomplish much. They look after the current
needs of their states or their districts, but they avoid anything
innovative or controversial. The quieter you are, the fewer
waves you make, the longer you stay in Congress. I did not
take polls when I was in the Senate, and I think it quite likely
that is one reason I am no longer there.

I wouldn't say I had a sense of mission; it just strikes me as
perfectly natural that it is rewarding to do something that you
feel is useful. Just to occupy an office and enjoy the perquisites
of being a senator seems to me to be rather a bore. Unless you
feel that you are doing something constructive in political
office, it's better not to be there.

What is so meaningful anyway about being in the Senate?
Or for that matter anywhere else? I have had discussions with
a close friend, a distinguished mathematician, about what it is
that motivates those highly intellectual mathematicians who
seem totally involved in their work to the exclusion of practically everything else. My friend told me about one fellow who
had isolated himself, wouldn't see anybody. They had to bring
food and leave it outside his door and knock, because he
didn't even want to see the waiter. When the waiter was gone,
he would reach out and bring it in and eat it. He stayed that
way working on some kind of theorem. Why, he was asked, did
he do it? Well, he thought, and he said he supposed it was for
the grudging approval of a few of his peers. That was about
it. It wasn't money. It wasn't anything else. It was just some
mathematical principle he was going to prove in the hope of
making an impression on a few colleagues and rivals.

Why, too, do some people become so absorbed in making
money? The answer, I think, is that they want that grudging

approval; they want to compel it by the power that a lot of money gives them. They are often disappointed in this hope. I've known some very rich people. On the whole they seem a rather frustrated lot, puzzled and disappointed by the lack of recognition that they feel to be their due. It may be different for those who inherit large fortunes. The ones who don't do anything for their money seem to rather enjoy it but are usually useless. They enjoy the comforts and the physical aspects of great wealth, but I don't sense any great satisfaction with their lives.

For many officeholders the satisfactions of office are more akin to those of the very rich than to the mathematician's. They can usually gain some measure of approval, or at least deference—grudging or otherwise—as long as they avoid outrageous scandal. But not very many have a theorem to prove. What they do have, and cherish, are perquisites. They protect them by assiduously avoiding controversy. And they retain office because no prospective opponent can think of anything really effective to say against them.

I have always been uneasy and uncomfortable with group thinking. I think Alexis de Tocqueville was right in his observation about how little criticism of the conventional wisdom is tolerated in this country. Majority opinion has a stifling impact on genuine independent thought. It's not that the majority says in a democracy, " 'You shall think as I do or you shall die'; but [it] says, 'You are free to think differently from me and to retain your life, your property, and all that you possess; but you are henceforth a stranger among your people. . . . You will remain among men, but you will be deprived of the rights of mankind.' "*

I have felt instinctively that if you become really intimate

*Alexis de Tocqueville, *Democracy in America* (New York: Knopf, 1945), p. 274.

with a group, then you start to adopt their ways, become involved in what has been called "group-think." Then your independence of thought and action is curtailed and your imagination stifled. You are restrained by peer pressure. If you really wish to be independent and make your own judgments about everything important, it is difficult to be a good team player—because a team has different criteria for making judgments about an issue. It's a matter of temperament, I guess. If you wish to merge your personality into a group and then try to persuade the members of that group of one thing or another, perhaps that is one good way to approach questions of policy. But that was not my natural way.

I was ambivalent about being a part of the administration of the Senate. I never aspired to be whip or majority leader. I didn't feel that I was clearly out of bounds, but even as chairman of a major committee I wasn't really part of the inner circle of the leadership of the Senate. Naturally you want to get along with your peers; I was always quite friendly with the leadership, but I never felt frustrated at not being an intimate member of that group.

I did not join the Council on Foreign Relations, even though at one time it was the center of the Old Guard establishment, including such luminaries as Dean Acheson and Robert Lovett, who had been secretary of defense, and their predecessors. They could call upon the president and make suggestions, as some of them did in 1960 to urge Rusk's appointment as secretary of state. They had that sort of influence; they knew the most powerful people, had a lot of influence through their associations. Even with such high-powered luminaries as Henry Kissinger and Cyrus Vance among its current membership, I think the council has lost much of its prestige. In any case it is difficult to retain one's independent judgment, perhaps even one's capacity for objectivity, as an active member of such a group. For my own part, I wanted to keep my own independence. You go into such groups and you can't help but be influenced by their talk. It becomes difficult to believe that such confident and successful people can be mistaken about anything.

I am reminded of the explanation offered by John Erickson, my former administrative assistant who went to work for Ford Motor Company, as to why automobiles in this country never kept pace with the innovations when the German and Japanese cars came along. The managers and executives of the big three automobile producers all belonged to the same clubs, played golf together, talked together, encouraged each other in the conviction that what they were doing was the best. In the meantime the Asians and Europeans made great innovations and left them behind. They very nearly went broke. If you associate with those people and think they are nice, as they often are, if you enjoy their company and are persuaded and encouraged by their views, you start to share their assumptions. You can't help it.

I simply didn't think that would do me any good.

You can't confront head-on every unpopular issue of your time. Civil rights was an issue I felt unable to confront. I began to acquire the thoughts I developed about the issue of civil rights and representation as a result of campaigning in the delta, where the blacks predominated. In a 1946 speech in Chicago I said that I would go along with the majority view of my constituents on certain local issues within their personal experience, but that on national and foreign-policy issues that were beyond their experience, such as supporting the United Nations, I would exercise my own best judgment and do what I felt was wise, regardless of the political consequences. Specifically, I said that I would support the poll tax, which was at that time a symbol of segregation. It was the device used to exclude blacks in the South from voting, and it was widely used in Arkansas. In a few cases, the big planters, if they wanted to carry an election, would pay poll taxes at a dollar a head and vote all the people on their plantations. Well, the blacks didn't know how they had voted. They went along, or had to go along, with what the boss wanted.

But in most cases, the blacks did not vote at all. The Democratic primary was considered much like a private club. The laws of equal treatment didn't apply to a primary. In the general election, that was another matter; you couldn't restrict their vote in a general election. But in a Democratic primary you could, and that was the most important—the only important—election at that time in Arkansas.

During my thirty years in the Senate, I never supposed I could take a leading or creative role in more than a few areas of public policy. I tried to be quite clear about what this meant from the beginning of my Senate career. If you oppose your constituents too directly on an issue too close to their hearts, you are not going to get elected. I realized early on, and still think it true, that there are things beyond their daily experience that they know very little about—such as, in general, foreign affairs. I felt there were issues fundamental to this nation as a whole in foreign policy that I wanted to focus on, and these were for the most part beyond the experience of my constituents. I thought it was my duty to speak out, to try to persuade my colleagues and constituents and people in general, and I felt I had a good chance to do so. Perhaps this sounds very elitist, but it is true nonetheless that most people do not know very much about Vietnam or Russia. They read the papers and watch television. But these are often very inaccurate, or flamboyant and sensational.

On questions such as the cotton program in Arkansas, or agricultural policies in general, you don't presume to tell the farmers that such and such a policy is not to their benefit.

You'd be a fool to do that. Often you don't know as much about it as your constituents do. You hesitate before going too directly against local projects and issues. It is no use trying to represent people when you are not willing to give credibility to their views about local conditions.

Besides, you are in a much stronger position to go to a local area and say, "Look, I'm talking about our relations with Japan or Russia or China. We've had these hearings on them and here is how I see the situation." Now you can stir up plenty of controversy on such issues, but your constituents are not in quite as strong a position to challenge you. But then you might tell them, "Look, you ought to integrate your schools; it won't hurt your children." I couldn't—I knew couldn't—convince them of *that*.

In those days in Arkansas my constituents were not about to be persuaded on civil rights. I could try to persuade them on subjects they didn't feel directly, immediately, emotionally attached to. But against an emotional fear like miscegenation, I don't think I had a real choice. I mean, what used to really bother them was the prospect of their young daughter marrying a black man. They couldn't tolerate the thought of it. That was what was in their minds, what they talked about. That was the way the fears were manifested throughout the delta region of Arkansas.

They did not always like my unwillingness to adapt to the majority view on foreign relations. But they went along, and I found many occasions on which I could get a receptive audience for my views. There was a tradition in the South in those days of keeping their senators in office, giving them more leeway than in other parts of the country if they had controversial views on some subjects. Perhaps I benefited from that.

Of course, I was obviously tempted to vote the other way on civil rights in my years in the Senate. I could have voted the other way in the 1950s, or followed the example of Representative Brooks Hays in the Little Rock school crisis in 1957—and retired from the Senate.

What happened to Hays did shock me, though. In 1957, as everyone remembers, President Eisenhower nationalized the National Guard after Governor Orval Faubus blocked the court-ordered integration of Central High School in Little Rock. Faubus was a very popular governor, approaching the end of his second term, and by no means at that time a demagogue on the race question. But there was a two-term tradition for governors in those days, and Faubus very much wanted a third term. I have little doubt that his motivation in opposing the integration of Central High School was political. And of course it worked.

I was in England at the time. People—including my elder sister, whose views I greatly respected—criticized me for not opposing Faubus publicly and taking a stand. I can't imagine what I could have done to oppose Faubus successfully; he went on to be elected four more times. And his main strength was that he had stood up for the people of Arkansas against the federal government's intervention. I knew it would be highly dangerous to get involved. So I avoided taking a stand. I could have committed political suicide very easily.

Brooks Hays, the local congressman, took what I would call a quite neutral stance, acting as a mediator between Eisenhower and Faubus in setting up a meeting between them and generally appealing for calm. As a result of that, in the election that followed shortly thereafter, he was defeated by a segregationist write-in candidate—which was unprecedented. I don't think it had ever previously happened in Arkansas history that a write-in candidate who was not the candidate of either party defeated a sitting congressman.

Brooks Hays was a charming fellow, and very popular. He led the biggest Bible class in Little Rock—it was even called "the Brooks Hays Bible class"—in the Baptist Church, which was one of the main sources of his political strength. He was a lovable character. It was a great and painful surprise to see him removed. Brooks used to tell a story about the old lady who approached him after the election and more or less apologized for having voted against him, explaining that if she had known it would defeat him, she would never have voted against him! He used to tell that story on himself. "I'm so sorry, Mr. Hays, I voted against you. I had no idea it would defeat you." I think that was true; a lot of people were just showing their disapproval, to sort of slap him down even though they really liked him. Even the people who voted against him were shocked by what happened. The issue has subsided in emotional intensity now, but in those days it led to the most extreme kind of demagoguery.

If I had criticized Faubus or issued a statement, I wouldn't have altered his course—other than to give him a reason to challenge me in the 1962 primary and to destroy me politically, which he clearly could have done if I had taken that stance. It's a question of how far you go and your timing. If you do it too soon, as Brooks did, you're out. And once he was out, he couldn't do any more educating. He couldn't do anything about it. After that, he played no significant or interesting role in Arkansas affairs.

It may be a rationalization, but a number of southerners felt at the time that the best way to deal with the racial issue over the long run was through education, that the blacks needed most of all opportunities for education, improved economic possibilities, improved health care. We believed that lack of education was the root cause of their economic disadvantage. Education would help with better jobs and improve their lot.

Consequently, I did support federal aid to education in the 1940s, an act that was quite unpopular in Arkansas and the South. The legislation never did pass the House and become law until the 1960s. Obviously the conditions of the black people had to be improved. We could not go on with the kind of discrimination and the lack of educational facilities forever.

So by and large I supported my constituents' views on the racial matter. I decided, for reasons beyond this particular issue, that I wanted to remain in the Senate. I did not feel like giving up my career in politics because of it. I didn't think then and I still don't think it would have been possible to persuade the white people of the South in the forties or fifties to support integration of the schools.

When the Supreme Court ruled in *Brown vs. Board of Education* in 1954 against the "separate but equal" doctrine, there was great pressure on us southern senators to adopt a common position. In those days, we all used to gather in Dick Russell's office and talk over common southern concerns. That's where the Southern Manifesto came from—attacking the court decision and calling for legal resistance to it. On these occasions I engaged in—or succumbed to—"group think" about the South and its problems.

I opposed the manifesto as it was first formulated. So did Price Daniels from Texas. Lyndon Johnson took the position that, as majority leader of the Senate, he couldn't take a public stand, that he had to deal with the issue from a national perspective. The truth was that he didn't much favor the idea of the manifesto and was looking for an excuse to extricate himself from it.

Well, Daniels and I didn't want to sign either. But in the southern caucus, through several meetings, our colleagues went to great lengths to get our agreement, stressing the importance of unanimity. They asked whether there was anything we could suggest so that we could support it. I argued that the original proposal stated that we flatly refused to accept the Supreme Court's decision. Daniels and I insisted that we would oppose the decision only by legitimate constitutional means, that we would go along with nothing extralegal—no force or anything of that kind. They agreed to modify it. Neither Price Daniels nor I, nor probably a few others as well, was for the final manifesto, but we didn't want to desert the other senators, either. We hated very much to stand out against our colleagues from the South. There was a sense that we were the poor part of the country, that we had historic reasons to band together against northerners who were again imposing on us. Much of that has changed now, but it was a palpable pressure in those days.

I don't think that the "gradualist" school that I belonged to, looking back now, will receive the approval of history. It was discredited by those who were for the legislation that directly attacked the civil-rights injustices. Those laws certainly did help. They should have passed. But I also believe that the gradualist approach was not without merit.

The South has profited by the successes of the civil rights movement; the situation is better than it was. But we have still not solved the root problems. We still have the serious problem of inferior education, which afflicts many Americans, but especially black people. Widespread discrimination remains, partly because so many blacks as well as whites are not educated, and this in turn is the real cause of the poverty, the low scales of pay, the crime. Civil rights declared black Americans to be equal; they were able to use public facilities. That is all to the good. But discrimination is still built deeply into our society.

Discrimination, like crime, education, and so many other matters of urgent concern, is unlikely to be addressed successfully until we devise a more effective means than we have now of putting leaders of genuine distinction in high office—men and women of intellect and character, of judgment and probity. The way we now choose our leaders is, to say the least, irrational. Substantive debates are rare and superficial. The process drags on too long. Other nations are able to choose leaders in four or five weeks, while we do it in two years—two years of unedifying maneuvering and feverish manipulation at extravagant cost.

Our electoral system has been demeaned and trivialized. Television, the PACs, the transformation of our party system—and, above all, the squalid political-advertising industry—are turning the business of democracy into a kind of farce. I don't think most people give serious attention to politics, which in its current degraded condition scarcely warrants attention. Electoral politics has become a kind of show; our elections have become a form of entertainment, although not very good entertainment. The candidates are cast in the roles of unpaid characters in a great television soap opera. And it is one of the curses of our political system that there always seems to be an election of some kind going on.

Candidates conduct very superficial debates; TV requires them to be short and snappy because it emphasizes the entertainment—as distinguished from the educational—side of debate. If you're not entertaining, the audience loses patience with you. If you don't know how to make one-liners, you're a failure. If you don't come on "human" (in the last campaign a euphemism for incoherent), you are a likely loser. Our recent president was a master of that degraded art, and the skill contributed mightily to his domination of American politics for almost a decade. Television, nonetheless, trivializes the candidates and politics in general. If a candidate tries to develop or argue a reasonable point of view in a logical, coherent way, he incurs the stigma of being "not very exciting," a tedious drone who bores people on television. Americans used to listen to and sometimes digest full-length speeches in the old days, but now they are fed a junk-food diet of heartburn-inducing TV "sound bites."

It is quite unpleasant and impersonal to have to make your principal presentations in a studio and have someone tell you when to stop and start, as opposed to the old way of speaking to the constituents directly, but that's considered passé now. When I first campaigned for office in Arkansas, I never had a big crowd—you didn't expect one. Very often, visiting a number of small communities, you would make eight or nine speeches a day and not have over twenty-five, thirty people, maybe fifty people, at any one event. Then usually on a Saturday night you would come into your biggest town and you might have two or three hundred. That was considered terrific. It was direct communication.

Perhaps I'm just not comfortable being on television. During the televised hearings on Vietnam in the sixties and seventies, Betty used to say to me that I looked too grim when I was conducting a hearing, that I looked mad. Couldn't I smile? I told her I couldn't smile when I was trying to think. She thought I was too abrupt with the secretary of state. I ought to smile. And I agreed—in principle. Some people like Jerry Falwell can smile all the time. They've got a built-in smile. Now, when I'm trying to concentrate, I apparently look grim. Is that so unusual?

I never was mad at Dean Rusk. I was just trying to concentrate. I was conscious of the fact that some of those people—I mean Rusk, and later Nixon's secretary of defense, Melvin Laird, to cite two notable examples—were expert at diversions. You'd ask them a question and they wouldn't answer it directly. They would go all around and talk about something else. It was very difficult to keep in mind what you were asking and make them come back to it. A clever man can divert you, lead you off the track—which they intended to do much of the time. They were very resourceful in avoiding answering your questions. It wasn't easy to keep asking your question to the point where they eventually got embarrassed about evading the issue and then finally gave you an answer. And that's a rather grim task, is it not? You can be pleasant if you don't take the hearings seriously, if you don't care if they answer or not. You can smile all the time, if that's your approach.

The media, moreover, to my considerable frustration, declined to cover certain important hearings—such as the re-examination of détente that I conducted in 1974. The media often cover only fragments of these public proceedings, which are, after all, designed to inform the general public. A super-star can always command the attention of the press, even with a banality. An obscure professor can scarcely hope to, even with a striking idea, a new insight, or a lucid clarification of a complex issue. A bombastic accusation, a groundless prediction—or best of all a "leak"—will usually gain a senator his heart's content of publicity; a reasoned discourse, more often than not, is destined for entombment in the *Congressional Record*. A member of the Foreign Relations Committee staff suggested that the committee had made a mistake in holding the détente hearings in public; if we had held them in closed session, he observed, and leaked the transcripts, the press would have covered them generously.

The problem for the Congress, for a senator, is not simply one of being heard. If you can produce something colorful, scandalous, turn it into a confrontation with an administration official, then you have a chance with the media. But if you try to interest them in an idea, a thoughtfully expressed view-point, a reasonable rebuttal to a highly controversial presidential speech, nothing comes of it. The hearings of the Foreign Relations Committee during the Vietnam War got attention if prominent officials were involved, but other hearings held in those years—one that probed into the psychological dimensions of our anticommunism, for example—remain a well-kept secret. If you want an idea brought to public attention, you must have a head-to-head confrontation with some leading official from the executive branch, and even then the idea is likely to be drowned in the spectacle.

Television has fed this tendency to personalize everything. It is all but impossible to convey an idea without having it personified, without making it critical of someone. The concept of an adversary, of fighting, seems bred into our television and newspapers. And if it isn't there, they'll put it in whether it was intended or not.

They cannot take a serious subject, like our relations with Russia, and give it serious discusion, unless an individual gets caught up in the question in some spectacular way. The views that are offered are usually superficial, often cynical. Comments by professional polemicists like George Will or Jeane Kirkpatrick about how you can't trust the monstrous, fire-breathing Russians are not serious discussion. Accusations of unpatriotism drenched in scorn are a means of stopping debates, not of starting them. And if you try to be serious anyway, you'll all too often find yourself labeled naïve, dismissed as being ignorant of the "hard realities" of life and of the world.

What I especially deplore in the media is the shifting of the focus from policies to personalities, from matters of tangible consequence to the nation as a whole to matters of personal morality or character of uncertain relevance to the national interest.

We used to make this distinction. Our focus during the Vietnam hearings was different: it was sometimes evident in those hearings that facts were being withheld or misrepresented, but our concern was with the events and policies involved rather than with the individual officials who chose—or more often were sent—to misrepresent the administration's position. Our concern was with correcting mistakes rather than punishing those who made them.

It is always a matter of relative emphasis. But since Watergate, the balance has shifted decisively. The media have acquired an undue preoccupation with the apprehension of wrongdoers, a fascination with the singer to the neglect of the song. The result is not only an excess of emphasis on personality, but short shrift for significant policy questions. I am not convinced, for example, that Watergate was as significant for the national interest as Mr. Nixon's extraordinary innovations in foreign policy. His détente policy was by no means neglected, but it certainly took second place to the news of Watergate.

Now this preoccupation with drama and focus on personalities has many aspects. But much of it flows from the simple fact that television is big business. It is a profit-making capitalist enterprise. Its purpose is to make money. The huge sums needed to run for political office, even at the state level, are tied directly to the costs of television—and a source of immense profit to the television industry. The ideal would be for the government to open up the airwaves to candidates for public office free of charge for purposes of serious discussion. Television today is not run in the public interest; it is run in the individual owners' interests. The stock of CBS or ABC or NBC goes up to $150 or $200 per share because it makes money. And it makes money because it charges enormous fees for thirty-second spots. It is hardly used for any educational purpose at all; public television is used for educational purposes part of the time, but it is not well financed.

In 1970, I proposed legislation designed to break the president's virtual monopoly of television access to the American people by requiring that the national networks provide as a public service a reasonable amount of time for congressional responses to presidential statements. The television people were all opposed, although today they do provide some time for congressional response through informal arrangements.

It is not enough. The means by which we choose our principal leaders should not be hostage to the self-interest of privately owned television companies primarily interested in making money. This is especially so when the license to use the airwaves is given them without real cost. Running for office through our unwieldy electoral procedure has become so costly that responsible, intelligent citizens without great financial resources are discouraged from subjecting themselves to the ordeal of a major campaign. In 1988 former governor Ruben Askew of Florida, for example, declined to pursue his candidacy for the Senate, declaring that he had learned that senators have to spend three quarters of their time raising money to pay the expenses of their elections. For similar reasons, six incumbent senators have recently decided not to seek reelection, some of them generally considered to possess superior ability.

As matters stand, television, with its heavy emphasis on image and entertainment, and with its enormous costs, has distorted and demeaned the electoral process. Television of course is used in countries with parliamentary systems too, but in some of these countries, where election campaigns in any case are confined to four or six weeks, there are effective checks on media abuse related to the way leaders are chosen and how television time is allotted.

With strong and intelligent leadership, especially with a president who is able to look at our problems objectively, I think the situation could be changed. The power of the president, combined with television, can be very great—for good or evil. In its short history, television has been used to distort the politics of our democracy, but that is not inherent in the nature of the medium or inevitable. It can just as well be used productively, creatively, and educationally. Like so much else that needs doing in our society, the first requirement is intelligent and sensitive leadership. Everything therefore comes back to the way in which we find and then choose our leaders.

3

VIETNAM REVISITED

If I went along with my constituents' beliefs on the racial issue, I did not do so in other areas. And this was particularly true in foreign affairs. Nowhere was this more the case than with Vietnam.

Vietnam was a major tragedy. When you strip away all the grandiose principles, geopolitical theories, and analogies that dominated American policy, you are forced back upon the merits of the case. And with Vietnam there never were many, if any at all.

I rarely thought about Indochina before the early 1960s. The war rather crept up on us without anybody knowing anything about Vietnam. I certainly didn't. Vietnam at that time was just a remote corner on the map of Southeast Asia. What little I knew had been about "French Indochina." I thought the conflict in that distant corner a minor thing compared to the danger of losing western Europe or of having a war with Russia in the late 1940s and early 1950s. As late as the early 1960s, we were primarily interested in the Senate in the question of Germany and Berlin in Europe, and of Cuba and Latin America.

When President Kennedy came to office, there were fewer than one thousand American military personnel in Vietnam. They were there as advisers and were not supposed to be involved in combat. I don't think anybody in Congress paid much attention to Indochina at that time. None of us on the

Foreign Relations Committee, to my knowledge, had ever been there.

By 1964, however, it became clear that the situation was rapidly deteriorating. On August 5, President Johnson called me and the other congressional leaders to the White House to tell us that North Vietnamese naval vessels had flagrantly and without provocation violated the freedom of the seas and attacked two of our destroyers in the Gulf of Tonkin. We were told that this situation demanded an urgent, prompt expression of national unity at a moment when we believed the country had been attacked. The president's attitude, apparently, was that if Ho Chi Minh saw that there was determination and unity on our part, he would sue for peace, come to a conference, and settle the whole matter by negotiations. That was the basic premise and justification offered by President Johnson for the Gulf of Tonkin resolution.

In retrospect I am all too well aware that it was a great mistake to be taken in by this presentation. But Congress had had a long history throughout the cold war of acquiescing to the executive in any seeming or alleged emergency. That was part of the problem of our gullibility. Very few thought at that time that we were being lied to.

The Tonkin resolution was drawn up and submitted to Congress by the executive. It was submitted first to the House, where it passed unanimously, and then brought to me as chairman of the committee to introduce and process in the Senate.

In retrospect I clearly made a mistake. I should have held hearings and gone into the issue carefully. The argument was put to us, however, that the whole thrust of the resolution was psychological, that any appearance of disunity or hesitation would undermine the goal of making the strongest possible psychological impression on the North Vietnamese. The resolution was presented as a way to peace, not war.

We were also in the middle of the presidential campaign of 1964. I thought Johnson was a peacemaker. He had spoken against sending our young men to Vietnam. I thought of Goldwater, on the other hand, as the gunslinger who was threatening to drop the atomic bomb. All of that undoubtedly colored my attitude. To hesitate, to question the administration's proposal, would give the appearance of undermining the president, of disavowing the nation's leader. And there I was too, the principal organizer of Lyndon Johnson's election campaign in Arkansas. We had greeted Ladybird in the state, set up the usual meetings, done all the things you're supposed to do.

The Senate Foreign Relations Committee in 1967 conducted an exhaustive inquiry into the events of August 1964 in the Gulf of Tonkin. This investigation showed conclusively that the administration had already, by the time of the Tonkin resolution, determined their policy. They had already decided that if they had to, they were going to intervene and use whatever force seemed necessary to subdue Ho Chi Minh, prevent him from taking over all of Vietnam. They were only looking for an opportunity to get the cooperation of Congress. When these alleged attacks took place in the Gulf of Tonkin, they found their opportunity.

They misrepresented the actual event. They knew there had not been an unprovoked attack. I am sure too that they knew there had been provocation by the South Vietnamese that could lead to some kind of retaliation. And they knew that this so-called attack was something less than an attack. The facts were such that Johnson should have known that, although I cannot say for sure what was in his mind. But the account presented to us was a misrepresentation of the facts for which the president has to be held responsible. Later, when Admiral True send me a telegram saying he suspected the entire account of the attack, based on what he knew from commanding destroyers for some twenty-five years, that the whole thing smelled suspicious to him, we initiated the hearings that discredited the official account that had led to the Tonkin resolution.

Only when we began those later hearings on the Tonkin Gulf did it really begin to dawn on me that we had been deceived. And I have had little confidence in what the government says since then. I know I should have been more skeptical. If I had known it was a fraud and a lie in the beginning, I would certainly have acted differently. I would have held hearings. But I think too that Lyndon Johnson would have gone ahead anyway, that he was just looking for the occasion to proceed with what he was determined to do.

There was almost no debate in Congress on the Tonkin resolution. When Senator Gaylord Nelson of Wisconsin offered an amendment to declare it to be our policy to avoid a direct military involvement in the Southeast Asian conflict, I said that I thought his proposed amendment was an accurate reflection of the president's policy, but that if I accepted it the resolution would have to go to a conference with the House to reconcile the two versions. The preoccupation with a resounding affirmation of our unity overrode considerations of legislative accuracy and precision. So the administration argued, and I fell for it. They told me that delay was unacceptable, that it would destroy the whole thrust of determined and united action.

In the beginning—before Vietnam, that is—it never occurred to me that presidents and their secretaries of state and defense would deceive a Senate committee. I thought you could trust them to tell you the truth, even if they did not tell you everything. But I was naïve, and the misrepresentation of the Tonkin Gulf affair was very effective in deceiving the Foreign Relations Committee and the country, and me, because we didn't believe it possible that we could be so completely misled.

Senator Wayne Morse of Oregon and Ernest Gruening of Alaska did vote against the Tonkin resolution. Wayne was suspicious and he was willing, as few individuals are, to be aggressive and abrasive to his colleagues, or to presidents, when he believed the people's interest required it. He was a great debater, a gifted practitioner of an art form now in decline, and he retained an old-fashioned faith in government by discussion—and the place for that discussion, in his view, was the Senate floor.

Wayne liked to talk. He had a reputation for being very controversial on issues that aroused his ire, of which there were many, and he had by this time been very outspoken on Vietnam. Just why Wayne felt convinced as he did has never been clear to me. He never hesitated to filibuster bills he disliked in the domestic field, but he only asked for two hours on the Tonkin resolution. He never tried to delay it. If he had delayed it longer, I don't know whether it would have changed things or not. You never know whether he could have forced the committee to hold further hearings. Nevertheless, he was right and I was wrong in my judgment. I don't think he had solid evidence, but he didn't believe the attack had taken place as the administration described it. He just felt deep down that something was fishy, that it wasn't true.

I started to read up on Vietnam about this time in 1964. I read books by the French-born writer Bernard Fall on Vietnam and invited him to an informal meeting of the Foreign Relations Committee. There was a longstanding tradition in the committee never to have a formal meeting with foreigners testifying. We would invite them to conversations and coffee, but a noncitizen could not then testify. I read Jean Lacouture as well, and became increasingly concerned that we were becoming excessively and dangerously involved in Vietnam. In private contacts with administration officials, I began to urge that we withdraw.

After the 1964 election I became increasingly uneasy. There were signs of escalation. Throughout this period, Johnson was continually reassuring me. He spoke of his valiant efforts to resist extremist pressure for escalation. I had at that time great hopes for Johnson's domestic program; it really looked as though, after all these years of the cold war, we would seriously turn our attention away from the obsession with communism—to our sorely neglected domestic problems.

Then came the February bombings of North Vietnam in response to the attack on the American Army barracks at Pleiku. Lyndon called us together, in one of those leadership meetings with the chairmen of the appropriate committees, the leadership of both houses, the CIA, the chairman of the Joint Chiefs.

It was quite clear that he was contemplating a major escalation. His usual procedure by this time was to outline a course of action and then call upon the various people to say what they thought of it. He was feeling their collective pulse. But of course his real objective was to get them morally committed to his proposal before it was presented in Congress. He was trying to foreclose as much dissent as possible. I reckon that was his main motive.

John McCormack, Speaker of the House of Representatives, used to be the stalking horse. Johnson always asked for him to speak first. "Well, Mr. President," he would say in effect, "you know, you are the leader. We have great confidence in you, and whatever, whenever there is any question about a policy, about our strength, about supporting the United States, I am always for the strength of the United States"—and so on. "I am all for maintaining unity behind the president, behind the policy." McCormack would invariably support and agree with Johnson. It always ended up that he was completely in agreement with whatever the president was proposing in this area.

Then Lyndon would go down the line and, as often happened, Mike Mansfield, being the majority leader of the Senate, was called upon. Mike often came anticipating what was going to happen and in this instance had prepared a short statement. He was very reluctant to escalate our involvement and warned against it. Then I would speak. I said I agreed with Mike. I thought we ought to be very reluctant to send any more troops, to get any more deeply involved. I said that I thought the Tonkin resolution was designed to give support for the president to stop the spread of the war, and that with this affirmation of unity, he could negotiate and make a settlement and stop the war.

Mike and I were about the only two people in that group who did not support the president's evident beginning of the escalation of the war.

My suspicions grew, although I wasn't yet really very secure in my evolving views. I was just in the process of learning about Vietnam. In those meetings Lyndon did not act as though he minded my comments. I kept thinking that I could influence him privately. I saw him quite often. He was very friendly to me, and as long as I didn't make a *public* statement, he was willing to talk. Not only was he willing to talk, but he had Dean Rusk talk to me and he sent other people to talk to me. I kept thinking, as long as people were doing that, that one of these days I might influence them.

Lyndon would tolerate you telling him quietly in his office that you didn't agree with this and he ought to do that, and he used to argue with me. In fact, he would make you think he agreed with you. He kept saying he was seeking a way to minimize the war and not to expand it, and to find a solution and negotiate a settlement.

On April 5, 1965, I sent Johnson—and also McNamara—a memorandum saying that it was compatible with our national interests for Vietnam to be unified under the rule of Ho Chi Minh. I said that we would be much better off with a strong, independent communist country than with a weak democratic one that could not survive. In those days the real threat seemed to come from a militant China, and the premise of my memorandum was that by supporting a strong nationalist movement in Vietnam under Ho Chi Minh, we would restrain China from taking over Southeast Asia. Ho, I believe, was a true patriot, like Tito of Yugoslavia. I thought this more the more I read about Vietnam. I was not advocating a communist-dominated Vietnam. I merely proposed that we could *accept* it if it arose from the local power situation. If the administration was afraid of Chinese expansion, this surely was an appropriate way to deal with the possible danger. Ho, I thought—and so I argued—would run an independent communist state, just like Yugoslavia, a country to which we had given considerable aid.

It is quite possible that if Eisenhower, at the time of the Geneva Conference in 1954, had said that we would accept the agreement and let the proposed elections go forth, the whole course of our history would have been different. Eisenhower himself later wrote that, if the election called for in the Geneva agreement had taken place as scheduled in 1956, Ho would have prevailed by eighty percent of the vote. We had always professed to believe in self-determination and the right of every country to its own government. What we did after Geneva was to deny that, because it didn't suit us. It was a great mistake. Ho would have won; the brutalization that later took place because of the war would not have occurred. The Vietnamese might not have been our friends, but they would have been independent.

Lyndon didn't respond to my memorandum of April 5. He

usually didn't respond to those memos. When you saw him later, sometimes he would raise the subjects you had addressed and acknowledge them—up until my speech in September 1965 on the Dominican Republic.

At this time too President Johnson was preparing a speech on Vietnam to be delivered at Johns Hopkins University in Baltimore. On April 6, 1965, he asked Mike Mansfield and me to come down to the White House. Looking back now, I can see that he was making an effort to persuade us to come along, to get on board, as he would say. He read us the speech—gave us a copy to read over there in the Oval Office. What were our suggestions? Well, we made a few, a word here and there, trying to moderate it, to make it a little more conciliatory.

In response to the president's gesture of consultation, I made a speech in the Senate praising his effort, supporting his apparent willingness to negotiate or suspend the bombing. I thought I would respond to him by being encouraging. The changes we had made were not much, but they did moderate the speech.

On April 28, 1965, Johnson sent the marines into the Dominican Republic. He called us to the White House and told us that his sole purpose was to protect American lives and those of other foreigners. He said nothing of communist infiltration. The island was in upheaval, and American lives were endangered by the revolutionary movement and the threatened overthrow of the ruling junta by supporters of the former elected president, Juan Bosch, who had himself been overthrown by the junta then in power. But when the president spoke again, on national television of the evening of May 2, he abruptly reversed his rationale for committing twenty thousand troops—from saving American lives to preventing the expansion of communism in the Caribbean.

The Dominican Republic focused my attention more positively on our policy of intervention not only in the Caribbean but also and especially in Southeast Asia. I was already very concerned about Vietnam, and here was another example of what appeared to be a very precipitate and injudicious use of force far beyond what could be justified by the circumstance. It seemed to me wrong to send in twenty thousand soldiers, when all we were doing was intervening to thwart a revolution that was probably justified. Once again we were intervening to prevent the local people from changing a status quo they thought was quite unsatisfactory.

I found myself increasingly in opposition to what Johnson was doing. There was a combination of factors involved. Partly, you feel that you have been studying a problem and start to have some confidence in your own judgment. In the beginning these things seem so complicated that it is difficult to get at the root of the truth of the matter. When you start out on most of these foreign-policy issues, you don't really know much about them.

But it was not just that I was becoming more uneasy about Vietnam. I was more and more beginning to see that this habit of intervention by a great military power was not a good idea. The circumstances did not justify it—in Vietnam or the Dominican Republic. It was somewhat the same idea that I had had on the Bay of Pigs, though not exactly. Supposing you prevail—what are you going to do with Cuba? We had it once. It didn't work out too well. You've got to let these countries work out their own future, find the system that suits the people. You cannot impose it.

The closed hearings on the Dominican Republic that we held in the Senate Foreign Relations Committee in the summer of 1965 had a deep effect on my thinking. On the basis of those hearings, I made a speech in the Senate on September 15, 1965, analyzing the Dominican affair. That speech led Johnson to break relations with me. The evidence, however, was incontrovertible; we had intervened for the primary, if not sole, purpose of defeating the Dominican revolution, which, on the basis of the most fragmentary evidence, was judged to be communist-dominated or certain to become so. This panic over communism, this fear that the Dominican Republic would become "another Cuba," however, was based on no credible evidence. The point I made then is valid now—not that there was no communist participation, but "simply that the administration acted on the premise that the revolution was *controlled* by communists—a premise which it failed to establish at the time and has not established since."*

Perhaps I should not have gone public about the Dominican intervention; some of my most trusted advisers tell me that to the present day. But nothing I learned in those hearings made me feel optimistic about the kind of influence I could exert on Johnson in private. Some of my staff still believe that I failed to take advantage of a real opportunity to ingratiate myself with the president so that I could be more persuasive. Perhaps there was such an opportunity, if I had been astute enough, to cultivate him, and perhaps offset the influence of Rusk and McNamara and Taylor that finally prevailed. At the same time, I felt inadequate to do it.

Perhaps I should have flattered him more. It's not enough to deal with a highly emotional man without doing this, and Lyndon Johnson was an emotional fellow. He was brought up in the political school of personal relations; the issues were inseparable from the personal relations.

I had first become acquainted with Lyndon Johnson when we were both in the Senate in the 1950s, through Dick Russell, who was our mutual friend. Dick took Lyndon, who became the Democratic leader in 1953, as his protégé. Dick was chairman of the Armed Services Committee; he liked the substan-

*J.W. Fulbright, *The Arrogance of Power* (New York: Random House, 1967), p. 91.

tive legislation and, for reasons of his own, did not want to be majority leader, although he probably could have been.

When I became chairman of the Foreign Relations Committee in 1959, Lyndon was friendly to me. I had succeeded to the chairmanship much more quickly than normal, because more senior members were unavailable; Brian McMahon of Connecticut, for example, had died of cancer and Claude Pepper of Florida had been defeated in his reelection campaign in 1950. If Pepper hadn't been defeated, he would have become chairman. These are just the luck of the draw—pure coincidence—and so, for such reasons, I became chairman after having been on the committee for only ten years.

Lyndon was devoted to the business of the Senate. He had few diversions. He made it his business to know every senator, what they liked, what they didn't like. He was assiduous in his pursuit of power in the Senate.

We didn't share a social life; our relationship was friendly but professional. He didn't do anything I like to do. He didn't play golf or any games or anything of that kind, and I rarely saw him socially anywhere.

But politically I saw him practically every day, and he was very cooperative with regard to whatever I had to do professionally. If a bill came from the Banking and Currency Committee, which I chaired earlier, or later, out of Foreign Relations, he was very cooperative. He would always say, "Well, when would you like it brought up?" and so on. He tried to work with you. We got on very well that way. He helped to get your bills through, get a hearing on them. He had much to do with that as head of the Democratic Policy Committee of the Senate. The Majority Policy Committee is very important. It schedules which bills are to be taken up, and which are not; who gets an opportunity to get action and who does not. You can be shunted aside very easily, and it is very important to have the cooperation of the majority leader.

Lyndon was very good at flattery. That was part of the game. He flattered everyone. He used that expression to me: "You're my secretary of state." He didn't show much interest in the substance of a foreign-aid bill itself, or of other foreign-policy issues. His attitude was, "If you're for it, fine. You're my secretary of state." That sort of thing. Probably he said that sort of thing to everyone: "You're my secretary of the treasury," "You're my secretary of agriculture"—what have you. My guess is that was part of his routine.

I think Lyndon thought he had been very kind to me when he was majority leader, as indeed he had been. He used to take credit for getting Theodore Green to resign as chairman of the Foreign Relations Committee so that I could take his place. Green, who was ninety years old at the time, had begun to lose his hearing and couldn't follow the hearings very well. It had gotten embarrassing and Lyndon had intervened. Lyndon felt I was indebted to him, and when I later criticized some of his policies, I think he felt not only opposed but betrayed. So for my part I tried to keep friendship and issues separate. That is why, when I publicly criticized our intervention in the Dominican Republic, I wrote him a long conciliatory letter in which I tried to assure him of my friendship and respect. I just said that on this particular issue I didn't agree. But that was not the way he looked at it.

After that, Lyndon didn't have anything more to do with me. I saw him very seldom—only on official occasions after that.

I thought Lyndon was wrong to break this way. I thought he should have responded to my letter and shown a little more consideration of the fact that, as a senator, I had a right—maybe even a responsibility—to express my views and initiate a debate. So I didn't like it at all. But there was nothing I could do about it. He struck me from the White House guest list, and I felt he was making a personal issue of our differences over policy. I didn't expect that. I was naïve not to have expected it.

I remember my administrative assistant, Lee Williams, saying, "It's a serious mistake if you break with Johnson publicly. Then we won't get any more help out of the administration for our Arkansas projects, and politically that will be a great handicap to you." That turned out to be true. Lyndon could discourage those projects I advocated for Arkansas. Or, to put it another way, when you had something that you were interested in, specific cases, and you would take it to him, he could call up the budget director, for example. He would say, "I wish you'd look into this and if possible find a way to put it in the budget." And he'd do it. Oh, yes, it was very important to have a president call up the director of the budget and say, "Would you look into this and see if you can find a way?" It didn't mean he'd *do* anything, but it was very helpful. There's nothing like a little boost from the president to the director of the budget, then or now. Of course, if you are chairman of the Appropriations Committee, you don't need the president. You can call up the budget director yourself. It all depends on your position. Lyndon did help some before the Dominican speech, but never after that.

I suppose there was also a very basic difference of temperament between the two of us. Lyndon was a perfect example of power—physical power. He was big—physically he was a big, powerful fellow. He could intimidate nearly anybody, and he did. I think his record in Texas politics shows that. It was kind of a frontier state where money and power made the difference. It didn't depend a lot on issues of any kind—certainly not in foreign policy.

It was natural from his background to be inclined to believe that he could achieve his purposes by the exercise of military power. I simply feel that you can't. I had an older brother who was much more powerful than I was. I couldn't have survived

116

if I hadn't tried to accommodate. I had no possibility of getting my way with physical power, even as a boy. I had to adjust to greater physical power. I think maybe this led to a certain prejudice against intervention with force unless there is a dramatic reason for it. Lyndon was just the opposite.

I spoke to many of my colleagues in favor of a neutralized Vietnam. But even with those who agreed in private, I could not get far. Dick Russell himself (the chairman of the Senate Armed Services Committee) had reservations about the war. He used to say to me, sitting at lunch, that we should never have gotten involved there. He said he had told Eisenhower that it was a mistake to send those two hundred "advisers" after the Geneva Conference in 1954, that the involvement would escalate. But once we were involved, he felt we had no alternative. Once you made the commitment to go—so Russell argued—then you have to support the military. Although he would always repeat nearly every time the matter came up that he thought it was a great mistake to have become involved, that the original commitment was wrong, he saw no alternative once the military was committed. That kind of reasoning never did appeal to me. I used to say—paraphrasing Alexander Pope—that to admit a mistake is only another way of saying you are smarter today than you were yesterday. If it was wrong then, it's still wrong. There is no moral turpitude in admitting mistakes. But Dick Russell, for one, just could not see it that way.

I did not try to cultivate influential colleagues like Russell to try to present a unified viewpoint to President Johnson representing a consensus of those senators he had trusted most when he was in the Senate. With people like Russell, who was older and more experienced than I, it seemed to me presumptuous to try personally and privately to change their views. I preferred to make my arguments in speeches and in public debate for their consideration. I was always reluctant to try personally to influence my colleagues. I thought it would embarrass them, or offend them, if I tried to tell them what to do.

Russell, though, was very easy to talk with. And he was a great advocate of the democratic process. He thought every senator had a right to express his views. He always insisted upon it. He was very meticulous about the enforcement of the Senate rules, that you shouldn't shut off debate. He believed in the principle of unlimited debate. He thought senators ought to have the chance to do that, and he never indicated that anybody should be cut off from the debate. Johnson, by contrast, preferred private persuasion to the public discussion of differences.

I've always thought that the democratic process can stand a little difference of opinion. Johnson and others seemed to think that in foreign affairs, unity was essential, that we must show unity when under challenge, and in this way we would impress the Vietnamese. Well, it didn't. I don't think that there is much in that argument. A debate and making the right decision are far more important. To be united on the wrong course is certainly of no benefit to the country. The main issue was to try, through debate and inquiries, to determine what was the right course.

In the fall of 1965 I was scheduled to lead a Senate observers' delegation to the Commonwealth Parliamentary Association meeting in Wellington, New Zealand. Normally it is the prerogative of a committee chairman heading an official delegation to be assigned a White House jet aircraft. But in the wake of the Dominican controversy, President Johnson refused to let me have a jet and my delegation was forced to travel in a comfortable but lumbering propellor-driven DC-6 of World War II vintage. It was a long, slow trip, with refueling stops required on islands across the Pacific.

Johnson's disapproval of my actions was evident during the

trip. When we got to New Zealand the American embassy did not wish to provide even clerical services for me; they didn't want to reproduce my speech because it was contrary to official policy. I said that was all right, that I could find a reproducing machine, that we would have the Commonwealth Parliamentary Association reproduce my remarks. That was before Xerox. The embassy, however, finally agreed to do it.

In the course of that protracted island-hopping, I found the opportunity for long discussions with Senator Hiram Fong of Hawaii about China and his background as a Chinese-American. He was a very successful Chinese-American, a very strong individual who had done extremely well in Hawaii. I was also reading during the trip about the Opium War of the 1840s, and was becoming increasingly skeptical of the prevailing antipathy toward China—a vision that Rusk and others were using to justify our role in Vietnam. Their premise was that we were thwarting the expansion of an aggressive China. Senator Everett Dirksen, the Republican leader, used to say that if we didn't stop the Chinese in Vietnam, we would have to stop them in San Diego. The theme in those days was that this whole war was restraining the expansion of China, as the flag-bearer of the international communist conspiracy, and that China was a puppet of Moscow, and the Kremlin the source of all evil. In subsequent hearings before the Senate Foreign Relations Committee I found myself disagreeing completely with Rusk on these matters. And the more we argued, the more the differences grew. They didn't come together, they got stronger.

The conversations and my readings in the course of that long journey across the Pacific and back gave me the idea of initiating, when we got back, a series of public hearings on China and on the background of the war in Vietnam. Ostracized as I was, I had no further possibility—if ever I did—of influencing the Johnson administration through quiet persuasion. The available alternative was public education through the forum provided by the Senate Foreign Relations Committee.

I was especially concerned with the question of China, because it went to the heart of the rationale for Vietnam. The question was whether China was aggressive. I think the hearings that we began in the winter of 1966 paved the way for a quite different view of China. Prior to that time, China was being judged aggressive not on the basis of her actions, but because she was communist. This began to change after the hearings, in the course of which I concluded that our government had made a very serious mistake back in 1949 in refusing to recognize the new Chinese government led by Mao Zedong. There is impressive evidence that Mao would have preferred at that time to deal with the Americans rather than the Russians, but Acheson, Rusk, and Truman mistakenly judged, after the outbreak of the Korean War, that Mao and China were puppets of Moscow, and refused to recognize the legitimacy of the new government. This decision contributed substantially to a generation of conflict between China and the United States.

Sometimes, though, in the public national debate that began in that winter of 1966, the president and his advisers skipped the rationalizations about China and Russia and the communist threat, and simply said they had the requisite *authority* to conduct the war in Vietnam. Johnson carried the Tonkin Gulf resolution in his hip pocket, and every time he was challenged about Vietnam, he would pull out the resolution and say, "Here, look what Congress did." This spared him the necessity of going into the merits. He did not have to explain. He did not have to go into detail. He said, "Look, you authorized anything I wanted to do."

When Secretary Rusk came to the Foreign Relations Committee to testify, he would first try to justify the war by talking about the threat of communism and containing Red China, and when that began to be frayed by facts and events, he would go back to the Tonkin resolution and to the SEATO treaty. I said to him, "I do not believe the SEATO treaty ever contemplated any such action," but in his dogged persistence, all other justifications having evaporated, he would retreat to the Tonkin resolution or SEATO treaty, saying, "You passed it."

After my personal relations with Johnson were broken, there wasn't much else I could do but hold the hearings. I called them educational hearings, hearings to educate the Senate and the public about the substance of our policy in the Far East. I think they served a good purpose. We didn't have the kind of power wielded by the Appropriations Committee. You can't make anybody do anything in the Foreign Relations Committee. You could hope to influence policy only by marshaling facts and national perspectives through thorough and penetrating hearings.

From that testimony on China I think it became quite clear, to those who paid attention, that China could not be considered militarily aggressive, or to be threatening to take over all of Southeast Asia. We also heard authoritative witnesses on Vietnam, such as General Gavin, who validated my view that it was wrong to undertake the kind of mission we were engaged in in Vietnam.

In retrospect, as became clear in those 1966 hearings, the decision not to recognize China in 1949 was indeed a fateful mistake. We refused at that time to listen to those experienced, professional diplomats like John Service who knew China best, and whose reporting suggested the deep-rooted independence of the Chinese Revolution. We just couldn't say, "Well, we'll accept the revolution," just as we couldn't accept others.

That's what we refused to do too in Vietnam. The Vietnam

hearings showed that Ho Chi Minh had written to the State Department several times in 1946, pleading with us to assist him and saying he was modeling his constitution on our institutions. The Truman administration did not acknowledge his letters. What a difference it would have made if somebody had taken the pains to say, "Well now, this might be worth looking into," and if we had sent somebody to Vietnam or asked Ho to come over here. Those decisions were made with little if any debate, and reflected the almost instinctive anticommunist mentality that has so quickly taken hold since World War II. The State Department in the early postwar years under Acheson insisted that Ho did not represent an authentic government, that he was a rebel under the control of foreign masters, and that we did not receive communications from rebels, certainly not communist ones.

I don't know whether I was radicalized by the war as some commentators have suggested. Certainly I thought more and more about our global policy and about our anticommunist obsession. And the more I thought about it, the more I became convinced that that obsession had distorted our perceptions and impaired the judgment of our leaders. I was strongly criticized for having lent support to the antiwar agitation that began to develop in the schools and universities. I agree that the hearings did serve to legitimize protest, but the protest that we legitimized was peaceful and lawful. I believe that we helped, so to speak, to bring it in from the streets. That was a large part of what we *could* do.

The Foreign Relations Committee, as a forum of debate and dissent, removed the stigma of disloyalty from the raising of questions about the war and from efforts to end war and the advocacy of peace. That was the main function, the practical outcome. It was to make opposition legitimate within the framework of democratic institutions. Otherwise it might well have gotten out of hand—it surely would not have vanished—

and provoked in turn even greater measures of suppression than those that the Nixon administration employed.

I received numerous letters from students and from prospective draftees who were considering going to Canada, or to jail, to escape the draft. I always wrote to them, saying that as long as you live here, you have to obey the laws; that it was perfectly legitimate—indeed a measure of their idealism—to object and try to change the laws, but that as long as the law required them to do military service, they should accept that law. Otherwise they would be penalized and stigmatized, and their idealistic energies would be lost to the nation. That surely did not mean they ought not to argue that the war was wrong. That was a position that many of my colleagues never quite accepted.

Looking back at my role in criticizing the war in Vietnam after 1965, my only regret is that I was not more effective. I thought I was going quite far at the time. I was severely criticized for legitimizing the student dissent. Not many of my colleagues were very impressed by my arguments about criticism being a higher form of patriotism—the idea articulated by Albert Camus, that the highest form of love of country is the devotion we give not to our country as it is but to its highest ideals. I recalled too in those war years, and invoked, the insight offered by Adlai Stevenson in 1952 that "it is often easier to fight for principles than to live up to them."

It is a daunting task for an individual senator to publicly challenge the president of the United States, with the aura of power that surrounds him. It is difficult to mobilize the self-confidence and to feel the degree of conviction in your own mind that will enable you to go beyond a certain limit. There's always that nagging feeling that you could be wrong. You're never quite that positive. Only fanatics are that sure of themselves.

Looking back on the Vietnam War, it never occurred to me

123

that President Johnson was guilty of anything worse than bad judgment. He deceived the Congress, and he deceived me personally, over the Gulf of Tonkin episode and his purposes in the election of 1964. I resented that, and I am glad the deceit was exposed, but I never wished to carry the matter beyond exposure. I never had the slightest sympathy with those who called President Johnson and his advisers "war criminals."

For the record, I never considered President Nixon a "war criminal" either, although you can call Watergate a crime. I was not as outraged by Watergate as most of my colleagues were before it was over. The offenses involved were largely derivative—products of Nixon's effort to stamp out opposition to the war. Many presidents have done things that were legally not as bad but were substantively as bad or worse for the country. I didn't think Watergate should be passed over, but I didn't think either that it ought to be allowed to consume the country's political energies for a couple of years, as it ultimately did. I even encouraged Jack Javits in 1973, as I had encouraged Ralph Flanders of Vermont with respect to McCarthy in 1954, to introduce a resolution of censure. My thought was that the matter ought to be gotten over with as quickly as possible and that, since the perpetrator was a Republican, the leadership in setting it right would be more credible coming from a Republican. But Javits was not interested, although he later supported impeachment.

The worst thing Nixon did was to continue the prosecution of the Vietnam War. When he first came to office, I sent him a memo suggesting that it wasn't his original responsibility and that it would be to his advantage to bring the thing to an end. I talked with him and Kissinger in the White House soon after he came to office. He said he needed a few months to survey the situation, to evaluate the circumstances, to look into it. He left the impression that he was interested in what I had written to him.

On that occasion I left the Oval Office with Kissinger and walked back through the White House. The last thing he said was, "Well, after six months you will not be able to say we are following Lyndon Johnson's policies." That was, I thought, an oblique way of saying, "Yes, we are going to end the war." He didn't say it that way; it was an ambiguous statement. Nevertheless he obviously intended to make me feel that they were moving towards the ending of the war.

A short time later I had another meeting with Nixon. And this time I had some of those same feelings I had had with Lyndon. He made me feel, as I guess a lot of people do, that he was in agreement with me, but without specific promises or obligations. And so for a while thereafter I didn't say much in public—not until that fall of 1969, when Nixon announced what he said was a new policy, "Vietnamization." It was never a promising policy—reducing our military strength while pursuing the same political objectives Johnson had sought. It just widened the gap between the objectives sought and the means available for achieving them. So we went right back to where we were. And that interlude of believing that he was tending to end the war short of military victory was over.

That whole period seems very odd and elusive. The administration practiced a kind of expert manipulation that I would attribute in large part to Kissinger. They kept emphasizing that they were going to reduce the American troop presence, all the while obfuscating the situation and finally invading Cambodia. I had long since given up hope by the spring of 1970 and the invasion of Cambodia. I had given up the thought of working with the administration. It was once again a question of using the available means to reach the public, bringing whatever pressure we could to bring the war to an end. That is when some of us in the Senate started to examine the feasibility of cutting appropriations as a way to force withdrawal. The demagogues said we were voting to let our boys down—it was a very emotional time. In any case, we didn't have the votes—no more than twelve or fifteen votes at first. We used to gather together and talk informally about what could be done. But it was a daunting job to do more than education.

What a dismal period that was! You felt so frustrated trying to change that situation and being subjected to criticism from one side and then another. Everybody who didn't support the president and the war was made out to be disloyal. *Traitor* is about it. I wondered at those times how it would be to be a senator when the country wasn't in a Vietnam War. It must be rather pleasant.

We had the Pentagon Papers before they became public. The question was, what should the committee do about them? They remained classified. Should we get into a big row with Nixon over publishing them? We discussed the matter and decided it would be better not to precipitate a conflict over our right to publish them and divert attention from the main issue of the war itself. We were already in a very difficult period. I don't think they could have taken effective legal action against us, but it would have been damaging politically. Fortunately, the *New York Times* settled the issue by publishing them.

By then, I was not shocked by the revelations. The government, especially the CIA, had been involved in so many things—the misrepresentation was so common it was virtually routine. Not much would have surprised me by then. I thought there was no limit to what they were capable of doing.

126

The invasion of Cambodia was a dreadful act. As best they could, the Cambodians had maintained their neutrality; and our attack was inexcusable. But we did it, and the events that followed ruined Cambodia—and the consequences are still being felt in that part of the world. We've contributed to an awful lot of tragedy in the world.

I'd like to see the Vietnamese get out of Cambodia. Perhaps the Russians will play an effective mediating role. But I should think no one would want the Khmer Rouge back. It's a very difficult problem.

Even so, we should restore diplomatic relations with Vietnam. We ought to try to be halfway friendly to them, if we can. We ought not to be punishing them. Our conscience should impel us to conciliation at every opportunity. The argument that what happened since the end of the war shows the harsh, totalitarian nature of the regime we were fighting misses what is important. The real point is that what happened was largely the *result* of the war. It destroyed the old, traditional government and customs and practices. The war came close, politically if not physically, to doing what General Le May once proposed—bombing them back to the Stone Age. I think what has happened is a direct result of the war and of what we did in that war. If we had accepted the Geneva accords in 1954, Vietnam could have been an Asian Yugoslavia.

The question is, what have we learned from Vietnam? When you look at Nicaragua and some of Reagan's policies, the answer is, apparently little or nothing. Yet there is much that we should have learned, above all that we, as a nation, are no more immune than the great powers of the past from the arrogance of power. If we could begin really to appreciate what this means, we might start to turn away from the obsession with Russia and communism that has gripped us for over forty years, and at last confront what the futile quest for primacy has cost us. There is no greater human vanity than the belief that one's own values have universal validity, no greater folly than the attempt to impose the preference of a single society on an unwilling world. At the very least, this is what we should have learned from the tragedy of Vietnam.

4

Our
Militarized
Economy

The Reagan years were an irresponsible economic era. People thought the economy was doing relatively well, but they were wrong. We are emerging from a disastrous period, the culmination of longstanding tendencies towards the militarization of both our policies and our economy. Yet few of the experts—and with the notable exception of the Reverend Jesse Jackson and Governor Bruce Babbit in the 1988 campaign, few leading political figures—have been willing to raise the question of the militarization of our economy as the key to our global economic deterioration. The discussion has been on entitlements, foreign competition, the dollar, the balance of trade—all relevant, to be sure, but all related in one way or another to the politically forbidden topic of our militarized economy.

To question this militarization is portrayed as an attack on our very security and survival. It has become the sacred cow of our politics. You don't talk about it for fear of being accused of being unpatriotic, soft on defense. It used to be "soft on communism"; now it's simply "soft on defense."

The aura of patriotism stops debate; you're not really a patriot if you are not all for "defense"—or, more exactly, defense spending for overpriced, technologically sophisticated, often redundant, and sometimes simply unneeded weapons systems. It has become integral to the American political culture that advocacy of a militant, assertive position in international relations, of big defense, and, as they say, of

131

"standing tough" is identified with patriotism, strength, and virtue. Warnings against the danger of war, on the other hand, along with calls for compromise and negotiation, are, subliminally if not overtly, identified with effeminacy and weakness, cowardice and a lack of patriotism. It is a political handicap and a mark of guileless innocence to be for conciliation and the use of the United Nations to achieve peace.

Some years ago I participated in a briefing of new members of Congress and I was asked to explain my approach. Arms negotiator Paul Nitze was on the other side, advocating increased military spending and the need to increase and maintain our military strength. It was a clear and, to the new members, apparently convincing presentation.

I made the countervailing argument that it is no longer rational, in the age of nuclear weapons, to anticipate a showdown of arms. I did not suggest that it could not come, but only that if it did come, it would be because—and only because—we had taken leave of our senses. My point was that there ought to be some other way. Then I outlined the ethos underlying the Fulbright educational exchange program and how it suggests that we can approach other people with a view to finding ways to adjust differences through negotiations and joint ventures. I said that I thought the differences between us and the Soviet Union were not all that important to the future of our own country or of the human race. Many of the things that nations have fought about in the past turned out, in retrospect, not to have been very significant.

At the end of the briefing a young congressman, a very bright fellow, said, "Yes, I'm impressed by what you say, but it's too complicated. How can I ever explain that to my constituents?" It *is* complicated, and it is not the traditional way. We don't have *time* in this modern age or the resources—with television time costing thousands of dollars a minute—to explain such things. A politician has to put his program in a slogan or a capsule. It is so much easier to say, "Strength! More money for bombs! More power! We've got to be number one!"

It discourages me profoundly to read day after day about the experts discussing the balance of military forces. They keep arguing about a few more MXs or a few less Stealth bombers, a few of this or a lot of that, employing a magnificently arcane vocabulary the purpose of which, I strongly suspect, is not to elucidate but to intimidate. It is true, of course, that most people don't understand the complexities of armaments, but the principles and realities underlying all that hocus-pocus are not nearly as obscure and incomprehensible as the strategic intellectuals would have us believe. But they have preempted the terms of debate so as to scare off the rest of us and convince us that only they—the experts—are entitled to talk about national defense, when it is just plain common sense that this great multiplicity of weapons is nonsense. As Mikhail Gorbachev and, belatedly, Ronald Reagan came to recognize, we have accumulated weapons systems far beyond their usefulness. They are redundant. Yet the defense experts talk about these matters seriously, indeed with the utmost gravity, and the newspapers dutifully and respectfully report everything those people like Richard Perle say, which is usually provocative and dangerous as well as erroneous. But the nonsense defines the terms of debate. And a serious discussion of what can be done to change the attitudes and the intentions of the two superpower countries towards each other is effectively squelched.

Do any of our political leaders dare to say, "Look, this arms race is absolute nonsense," that our perceived defense needs are built largely on fantasy?

Consider Star Wars. By my reckoning the so-called SDI is a fantastic concept suitable only for Hollywood. That sort of thing works fine in the movies, or in the early-morning television cartoons that are scrambling the brains of our children. It is a fantasy, nonetheless, I would not deny that the amount of money and talent being poured into SDI might develop some effective weapons components, involving lasers, particle beams, and so forth. I am not a physicist; I don't know which ones will be workable. But the idea that you are going to put an umbrella over the United States to protect it against incoming weapons is fantasy, pure and simple. There is a difference between the spinoffs from an enormously expensive research program and the creation of an umbrella, as they call it. I doubt it can even address the problem of missiles fired from a submarine in New York Harbor. It still baffles me that we have been willing to squander billions of dollars on SDI in the apparently sincere belief, unfathomable to me, that there is any possibility of gaining security from nuclear-weapons systems in the same way that, before the nuclear age, we sought security from our army and fleet and air force.

In the Senate Foreign Relations Committee we had long hearings on the ABM in 1970–71. On the basis of what we learned at that time, I am convinced that Star Wars cannot prevent fatal damage to our country in a nuclear war. Those hearings of the early seventies, preceding the negotiations of the ABM treaty, are still relevant. There is not much difference. There is greater sophistication of certain aspects of missiles. But the missiles just don't come in the way you would want them to in order to destroy them. It calls to memory the Maginot Line. It would have been a great defense system in World War II if the Germans had attacked the way the French expected them to. Head-on, they might well have repelled them. But the Germans did not cooperate; they just went around the end of the French defenses, and the Maginot Line never even came into service. I suspect strongly that the same thing would happen with SDI.

We ought to have learned over the years that if we confront

the Russians with a constantly escalating military race, they will feel they have to respond. For the last forty years, because of our technological superiority, we were the ones who were bringing forward the new weapons. After all, we dropped the first atomic bomb. We initiated MIRV, the Trident, the B-1 bomber. The Russians had nothing comparable at the time. We are constantly out front, and we take pride in our primacy—like being first to the moon. If we did not continue to initiate these new weapons systems, I think it likely that the Soviets would hold back too. The possibility surely seems worth exploring. As Gorbachev seems clearly to recognize, these costly weapons systems strain Soviet technology and have become a debilitating drain on the Soviet Union's resources. And no security for either side can come through such incessant inventions of new weapons systems. I know of no instance in human history in which mechanical means alone, no matter how ingenious, have kept the peace for long between hostile great powers. What one has invented, the other sooner or later—and usually sooner—will also invent or overcome.

In the past, both sides have approached SALT talks in the belief that they must come to the bargaining table weighted down with "bargaining chips," according to the self-defeating theory that you must arm to the teeth before entering an agreement to disarm so as to have the greatest possible leverage with your negotiating partner. Since both sides engage in the practice, the very prospect of arms limitations has the effect of accelerating the arms race, so that the final agreement—when there is one—can actually sanction a *higher* level of armaments than the putative disarmers started with.

I remember the debate over MIRVs in 1969. Senator Edward Brooke of Massachusetts offered a resolution suggesting that we hold back on the development of MIRVs until we had an opportunity to try to negotiate an agreement with the Russians under which neither side would develop MIRVs. The Nixon administration opposed the idea, and we went ahead and developed our multimissile rockets and the Russians did the same. We thus multiplied the lethality of ballistic missiles and created a major new obstacle to arms control.

I do not at all like to blame my own country; it is personally painful as well as unpopular to do so. But I am alarmed and offended by the destructive psychology of action and reaction in the arms race and of the mounting mistrust it provokes. All these various aspects—military and psychological—interact so as to reinforce the basic cold-war assumption that the Soviets can never be trusted, that they are determined to destroy us, which creates an atmosphere in which it becomes all but impossible to reach effective agreements. That is what has to be worked on—the *attitudes* on each side. What are we going to do about them?

We have become a militarized economy. The arms race has acquired a momentum fueled by enormous economic interests and provocative ideological rhetoric. Spawned by our global military involvement, the military-industrial complex has become a powerful force for the perpetuation of the arms race from which it so hugely profits. Millions of Americans have acquired a vested interest in these expensive weapons systems; they provide profit for large corporations and livelihoods for working people. The same people acquire, indirectly, a vested interest in the foreign policy that has committed us to a spiraling arms race with the Soviet Union, made us the world's major arms salesman, and committed us to the defense of "freedom"—very loosely defined—throughout much of the globe.

Dangerous as it is, the arms race is also exceedingly profitable. It is profitable not only to "the Strangeloves of the military-industrial complex," as I. F. Stone called them, but to millions of honest, decent Americans whose primary concern is nothing more than earning a decent living for their families. The industries and businesses that fill military orders have become the largest single producer of goods and services in the United States.

Violence has become the nation's leading industry. It is not an enthusiasm for war but simple economic self-interest that has drawn millions of workers, their labor unions, and their elected representatives into the military-industrial complex. To those who build them, weapons mean prosperity, not war. For the industrialist they mean profits; for the worker, new jobs and the prospect of higher wages; and for the politician, a new installation or defense order with which to ingratiate himself with his constituents. These benefits, once enjoyed, are not easily parted with. Every new weapons system or military installation soon acquires a constituency—a process that is aided and abetted by the perspicacity with which Pentagon officials award lucrative contracts and establish new plants and installations in the districts of influential members of Congress.

Yet this militarization of the economy is undermining us internally. Weapons are not reproductive; they are sheer non-productive assets. They do not contribute to the welfare of the country in any positive way. On the contrary, they drain resources—human as well as material—that could be applied to making our consumer products competitive, or to restoring all the infrastructure that has been so rapidly deteriorating: bridges, railroads, highways, water systems, and above all, our sorely neglected public educational systems.

A powerful military establishment is relatively new to America. Prior to World War II we never maintained more than a token army in peacetime. In those days the military had little prestige or influence. Nor, in those days, was there anything resembling the military-industrial complex that looms so large today. Yet even before World War II you could see the presence of a certain or incipient militarism in Washington. Drive through the capital. Look at the number of statues honoring generals and military heroes. But where is the great monument to Woodrow Wilson, whose legacy to his countrymen and the world was the concept and promise of a world peacekeeping organization?

At the core of this new militarism is the professional officer corps made up of a few thousand high-ranking officers of unusual ability and energy. Marked as individuals of talent by their rise to the highest ranks through the rigorous competition of the military service, they bring to bear a strength of conviction and a largely shared ethos that give them an influence on public policy disproportionate to their numbers. Disciplined and loyal to their respective services, they operate with an efficiency and effectiveness not often found among civilian officials.

There is a danger that can arise from the narrowness of outlook of professional soldiers. Perhaps the critical deficiency in their outlook is a lack of empathy with the adversary, and a consequent deficiency of judgment in trying to predict that adversary's behavior. We have had great soldier-statesmen in the postwar era, such as General Marshall and General Eisenhower. But other, more typical military leaders who have wielded considerable influence have been characterized by a constricted point of view towards foreign relations—a viewpoint that takes little account of political complexities, less of social and economic factors, and less still of human and psychological considerations.

Over the postwar years enormous amounts of money have been made available and expended to disseminate the military's message and the Pentagon worldview. I looked into the Pentagon's multifaceted public-relations activities at various times in my Senate career and presented my findings in a book published in 1971 under the title *The Pentagon Propaganda Machine.* The campaign they developed in the late 1960s to sell the ABM system was also designed to shape public attitudes and, through it, public policy. The military does have legitimate need of an information program, but its legitimate purpose is to inform, not to promote political objectives. There is no need, for example, of self-promotional films for public consumption. Nor is there need to send military-sponsored speakers to address luncheon clubs and veterans' groups all over the nation. Nor is there need to set up expensive and elaborate exhibits at county and state fairs, or to take VIPs on pleasant cruises aboard aircraft carriers. Least of all is there need to have speaking teams crossing the country talking about the dangers of communism and the virtues of patriotism as they define it.

Compare the Pentagon's propaganda with that of our official propaganda agency, the United States Information Agency. Congress, wisely, has acted to circumscribe USIA's domestic activities. Only in the rarest of exceptions is it allowed to distribute materials within the United States. The far larger Defense Department, on the other hand, with far more people involved in public relations, operates without any control other than the permissive guidance of a benevolent executive, which is to say, without effective restraint, and it floods the domestic scene with its special, narrow view of the military establishment, its needs, and its role in the world.

I don't think it is the proper function of the military to determine or decisively influence our national priorities. Questions of the military budget as against measures to strengthen the domestic economy, or to control inflation, or to fund education, are properly vested in our civilian authorities, especially the elected representatives. I don't blame the military for giving their advice on how they see their mission. They usually ask for every conceivable contingency to be covered. The real criticism must be directed at the Congress and the president for their failure to reconcile all these considerations—the needs of our country and the probability of other countries responding to our arms buildup.

When Eisenhower gave his speech on the military-industrial complex before he left office, I wasn't as impressed with it as I am now. Of course, the problem has become so much greater. In retrospect I recognize that Eisenhower was remarkably astute about what was happening. I had started to be uneasy about where we were going about the same time. Much of the impetus for our great arms buildup, on top of Stalin's aggressive acts and brutal policies, arose from the Russians' launching of Sputnik in 1957. That event was a singular blow to our pride, an insult to our hitherto unshaken confidence in our great technological superiority. It appeared without warning and we were shocked—the idea of those backward peasants being able to put up a space satellite, even though it was no bigger than a basketball, a tiny little thing. But still it was a satellite, and we reacted as though they had spit in our face. During the 1960 campaign Jack Kennedy made a major issue of the presumed missile gap. It was phony, but we fell for it and it gave impetus to the great buildup, as well as to the state of mind that carried us into Vietnam—and also the moon.

I for one was not particularly impressed with Sputnik. It hardly seemed dangerous, but our reaction was highly jingoistic, and our space program since has been dominated by military concerns. Similarly, the Apollo project to race to the moon struck me as a distortion of values and priorities. Such sums, it seemed to me, could be far more usefully applied to education, or to the alleviation of poverty. I was struck and dismayed at how easily huge sums could be obtained for space projects, while funds for work that might lead to tangible benefits, like improvement of our industrial productivity, were assigned low priority. Space, like armaments, thus became invested with an aura of urgency, and therefore of primacy, vaguely but strongly associated in the public mind with the nation's very survival.

In such an atmosphere, as the military-contracting scandals of 1988 richly demonstrated, questions of economy and prudential management are cast aside. The floodgates are thus opened for unbridled profiteering by arms manufacturers, military contractors, and the parasitic "consultants" who sell access and influence. As noted, many ordinary people as well as the great corporations benefit from the huge sums wielded by the military contractors, whose industry has become a huge part of our national economy. Congressmen compete to get more military contracts and installations in their states because of the amount of money these bring in. It is a direct infusion of money into their districts, from which they hope— and can usually expect—to reap a harvest of votes. In an earlier era, before funds were funnelled so largely through the military, the process of allocating federal funds was linked to internal and civilian needs, such as the development of natural resources or of river systems such as that of the Arkansas River. It had direct economic consequences—helped transportation, gave us modern waterworks and lasting improvements. But today you can't arouse any of the religious fervor for a river project that is readily aroused by a military base.

There is also a brain drain associated with the militarized economy. We have drained much of our best brain power out of the civilian economy into military research and development. Projects like SDI attract some of the best mathematicians, scientists, engineers. Thus it happens that intellectual as well as financial and material resources that might otherwise be applied to building a better life for our people are drained away, taking a steady, mounting toll on our national infrastructure—on the bridges and railroads and highways, on the civilian industries in which we are losing our competitiveness, and on our public educational institutions. The ultimate irony is that it is these forms of production, which we call our national infrastructure, that constitute the real, solid base of our national security.

In earlier years, we spoke a lot in this country about the need not to bankrupt ourselves, of the great strength we had because of our strong, balanced economy. The Reagan administration undercut that. Calling itself "conservative," the Reagan regime, in a veritable orgy of fiscal radicalism—or "voodoo economics"—poured funds recklessly and prodigally into the militarization of the entire system. By 1988 federal indebtedness was three times greater than in 1980, necessitating a daily interest charge of $586 million.

We put our brains as well as our money into developing a few select areas of technological competitiveness—those that have military priority. You cannot be serious about economic competitiveness in the world if the only way you can envision our economy functioning is through the channeling of our best resources into defense. Why is it that the Japanese outdo us in most fields of production, including automobiles, televisions, computers, and other high-technology products? The answer is that they do not divert their talents, as we do, into the military; they don't spend their money on global interventionism—they don't station their troops around the world.

The Japanese have simply applied themselves and produced better-quality products. They are criticized, fairly, for some of their exclusionary trade practices, but on the whole I don't see anything unfair about their superior efficiency. I don't see how it's unfair to produce a better product than we do. I don't think we can sell many—or any—automobiles to them. Why should the Japanese want to buy a car that is less well made, less reliable in performance, and less durable than one they make themselves at a lower cost? There is indeed a measure of unfairness in their reluctance to let us sell them things that we do produce more efficiently, such as beef and citrus and rice, but that is not our central problem.

And no, I don't think they should be pressured to spend more on their defense. We are doing too much globally—too much is being spent worldwide on defense. If the Japanese don't think it is necessary, why should they waste their money just to please us? It is said that they are getting protection free from us and can spend their money elsewhere. Well, I think we can cut back too, and if the Japanese then decide that they need a larger defense force, they will build their own. I am not very comfortable with the idea that we need to be more concerned with another country's defense than that country is itself.

We have spent something over four trillion dollars on defense since World War II, about half of that on the upkeep of our armed forces overseas. But at this stage the Russians are not the primary threat to our national security. The primary threats are the damage to our economy caused by huge budget and trade deficits and the disarray of our political system. For several decades, our priorities have been distorted from what they should have been. This did not come about through a careful, reasoned decision to sacrifice welfare to security. The decision was made over the years in the panicked atmosphere of perceived crises and cold war. What we need to ask ourselves now is why we have become so prone to prefer military expenditures over public schools, flights to the moon over urban development.

It was short-sighted and improvident to assume back in the sixties that we could wage the Vietnam War and at the same time raise the billions of dollars needed to rebuild our schools and carry out all the other commendable activities associated with President Johnson's "Great Society." The war undermined Johnson's domestic programs, many of which were highly beneficial. You cannot wage a war and also draw on the resources, spiritual as well as material, to transform your own society. And now we see that the expanding economy of the sixties was deeply intertwined with the intensifying militarization.

It would be bad enough if it were just we doing this—or just we and the Russians. But militarization has become a worldwide phenomenon. We are one of the major suppliers, if not the major supplier, of arms in the Middle East and throughout the world. It is a huge business, highly profitable to the suppliers. Even in the poor countries, the needs of the people provide feeble competition for the demands of the military for the allocation of meager resources. If a country becomes an enemy of its neighbors, they feel that they have to spend enormous resources on the military. Economic development is set aside, and available funds flow to the military.

I do not wish to be unduly critical; the military is a reputable profession. You need a certain amount of it to keep order, just as you need a police department. But we and so much of the rest of the world have become paranoid about it. Our world has been devastated by constant warfare in the last century, and all the conflict has culminated not in peace and stability but in a world divided between these two huge, rival, conflicting ideological powers, with a largely impoverished third world made poorer still by endemic strife and warfare. The nations that are prospering are those relatively few that are not so obsessed with military expenditures.

It won't take us much longer before we feel the full effects of this folly. Rome took three hundred years to decline and fall. It shouldn't take us nearly that long, if we continue to squander our resources. This remarkable, even precipitous decline in nearly all our indices of wealth and power, other than missiles and the military, over the last twenty years, is quite possibly unprecedented in history.

There is a kind of similarity in the fortunes of major powers that go up and down; they experience the arrogance of power and then they are subdued. Paul Kennedy explains the fatal cycle in detail in his recent book. If I may claim a certain primacy, I pointed to the same phenomenon in my writings in the sixties and early seventies (*The Arrogance of Power*, 1967, and *The Crippled Giant*, 1972). It is very hard to reverse such things, perhaps impossible. We are deep in the process of decline now. It is dramatically evidenced by the loss of much of the respect we once had from most of the countries of the world.

Twenty years ago, practically every country respected us. Even the Russians acknowledged that they envied us. Khrushchev said that he wanted some of the economic achievements we had obtained for his own people, and wanted to outdo us in economic development. Today, although they are reluctant to trumpet it, few of the world's leaders think highly of our judgment or of our policies. It is reflected in the votes in the United Nations. And you see it from our side in our avowed disdain for those votes, as if we no longer had that "decent respect for the opinions of mankind" commended to us by the founders of this nation. I don't think the world in general approves of our militarization, of our policies towards Russia, or towards the Middle East or Central America. I certainly don't approve.

You see this decline in so many ways—some subtle, some less so. It is manifest in the policies that led us to become the biggest debtor in the world. It is there in the growing dissatisfaction arising out of the increasing gap between rich and poor at home and abroad. You see decline especially in the loss of control over the budget. It is evident too in the subservience of our foreign policy to domestic lobbies—a striking sign of our inability to direct our own affairs.

I cannot overstress my deep conviction that the *real* danger to the future of our democratic system is internal. We are *much* more likely to lose our democratic system through printing money, radical deficits, inflation, and the distortion of our economic and political life here at home, than we are through any external aggression by the Russians. Our desire and determination to outdo them in these military expenditures is external in a sense, but it has a very grave effect upon our economy. Our subsidies and interventions around the world are vastly too expensive, and often ineffective as well. That's where we will suffer serious defeats, and in the deterioration of our own economy.

It is much more painful to pick up the pieces after a society deteriorates, or after the economy collapses into a severe depression. That disrupts everything. Nothing could be more welcome to those who wish to see the collapse of the western world. We will have discredited the whole concept of private enterprise and democracy if we allow our economy—as well we may—to degenerate into another depression like that of the 1930s. Then it won't matter much what the bureaucratic propaganda machine says. People will judge on the basis of what's happening. Rhetoric has a very limited, short-term value. If the facts and the example don't conform to the rhetoric in a period of great turmoil, it's rhetoric that goes down the drain—you can't change the facts if we go into a depression, no matter what the president says or what the propaganda is.

I fear that it might well take a full-scale depression to shake us up. It's a terrible way to do it. It's such a horrible injustice to the poor people of this country. The rich will find ways to adjust to it. They have money and property. But the poor people who are on salaries and pensions are going to suffer terribly if we have to go through another depression. It is a very unjust way to pay for this extravagance. It does not have to happen, but we will have to come to our senses, or it is all too likely.

In this context, to cut the defense budget today by twenty to thirty billion dollars is just a drop in the bucket. We should start by cutting fifty to a hundred billion, and raise taxes to substantially cut the budget deficit. The tax rate is way down from what it was in 1980. Reagan cut it substantially, especially for the rich. At least we should restore it to where it was before Reagan.

I am all too aware of the political realities. If Governor Dukakis had gotten up during the 1988 campaign and said that the defense budget should be cut by $100 billion (it is beyond my imagination that Bush would have done it), he not only would have been defeated, he would have been thought of as a candidate for St. Elizabeth's mental hospital in Washington, D.C. Yet the power of the president is about the only power that can be used to stop this prodigal military spending. That power is essentially one of educating the Congress and the people and making it respectable and legitimate to question the role of the Pentagon and the necessity of the continuation of the arms race. If the president were willing to take a position of commanding moral authority towards slow stopping of the arms race, I think he could do it, especially if he were popular enough and willing to expend some of his political capital for a surpassing national purpose. But if he declines to do that, if he fears he will lose his popularity because of it—or if he actually favors the arms buildup, as Reagan did for most of his tenure, and also has broad popularity, as Reagan did—the members of Congress will remain afraid for their own political fortunes and too timid to take issue with this program of a continued arms race. A lonely, courageous stance on an issue of this kind is all too likely to lead to a congressman's demise—and how well they all know it.

If we ever do confront the consequences of our militarized economy, it will not be enough to just curb the military expenditures. We will need too to transfer a vast portion of those funds into other, long-neglected sectors of the economy. But how do you get from here to there if you cannot even discuss the issues—if you cannot, without bringing all hell down on yourself, address the issue of militarization and its ideological partner, the fervent anti-Russian animus that permeates so much of our thought and action; and if we cannot face up to this arrogant sense of our own superiority, this assumption that it is our God-given role to be the dominant power in the world?

The idea of the Reagan era that "government is the problem" just isn't going to get us anywhere. In such a complicated society as we have, you have got to have some kind of responsible, representative national authority to define priorities and allocate resources. That we can "get government off our backs" and privatize everything is at best an illusion, at worst an invitation to rapacity by selfish private interests. Deregulation does not work well, as we have seen, for example, in the airlines industry or in the dissolution of AT&T. Our system of public transportation is disgraceful. We have effectively done away with rail traffic, especially passenger trains, in many parts of the nation, something that no other advanced country has even considered allowing to happen.

The idea that competition is the sole component of economic strength is an old one. In earlier, simpler days in this country it worked pretty well. Indeed, before we became so deeply involved in international affairs, our government worked well. Now we are part of a complex international economic system—but we lack an institutional context in which we can effectively shape a sense of direction and a sense of responsibility. The privatization of so much of our American way of life is a way of shedding any sense of responsibility for the welfare of the public. You can call the alternative socialism if you like; many ideas relating to social justice and a well-run society may be denounced as "socialism," the term being taken not as a bona fide political philosophy but as a term of opprobrium. I think it is a sign of immaturity and childishness when we dismiss uncongenial or unconventional ideas with epithets, and pretend to debate matters at that level.

I have suggested on various occasions over the years that every nation has a double identity—as a power drawing down its resources through the conduct of foreign relations, and as a society replenishing its domestic resources through the energy and inventiveness of its citizens. In recent decades we Americans have drawn dangerously deep upon our reservoir of economic, political, and moral resources. That is the waste that I have deplored and resisted.

The militarization of our economy is a phenomenal waste. Until its roots and full consequences are understood, it will remain hard for us to fully grasp what has happened to us and our potential. I still think, as I wrote in *The Arrogance of Power,* that there are two Americas. One is generous and humane, the other narrowly egotistical; one is self-critical, the other self-righteous; one is sensible, the other romantic; one is good-humored, the other solemn; one is inquiring, the other pontificating; one is moderate, the other filled with passionate intensity; one is judicious, the other arrogant in the use of great power. But the America I have believed in cannot last forever in a militarized environment. The greatest threat remains, as it so often has throughout history, from internal follies, not external enemies. The road of continued militarization leads to continued decline and breakdown, even as its advocates speak of strength and power. The alternative road is difficult and uncertain. But it remains the one that promises some hope for a more peaceful world and a continuation of the more admirable qualities of the American spirit.

5

INTERVENTION

P rior to World War II, the United States limited its foreign interventions—interventions, that is, in the internal affairs of other countries—almost entirely to our
declared sphere of influence in Latin America. Since World
War II, the United States has become a globalist interventionist power. As the greatest power of the postwar era, we acquired a tendency to think that we had a responsibility to
intervene and keep order, and to promote and carry out
worldwide programs of development and democratization.
An ideal was involved—but it was, I believe, a mistaken ideal.
We just could not do it. We did not have the experience, the
knowledge, or, ultimately, the power. As the great movements
of decolonization swept over the world, it slowly, painfully
became apparent that we could not intervene wherever we
thought we perceived an interest at stake or a threat to be
dealt with. But for a time the idea misled us, and to some
degree still does. Only through costly experience have we
begun to recognize that, more often than not, intervention has
been against our own best interests—and in many if not most
cases, too, it has not served a useful purpose in the countries
involved.

I often wonder why, during my years in office, I so often
seemed so out of touch with the majority of the Senate about
U.S. intervention abroad, and why my colleagues seemed less

153

concerned with the dangers of the arrogance of power. I have from time to time, somewhat but not entirely facetiously, said that maybe I am the heir of the South with regard to the Civil War period. I may have absorbed an attitude towards big powers and big countries that has its roots in my Arkansas cultural background. You were not inclined, if you came from Arkansas in the years when I was growing up there, to be very arrogant. We were poorer than almost anyone else and there was a tendency in much of the rest of country to look down on Arkansas as backward and uneducated. It seems logical to me that this should have had an effect on my attitudes when I considered relationships between the United States and smaller, underdeveloped countries.

Because I grew up in Arkansas, I had a sense of what exploitation by the rich states was all about. Some of the major resources of my state were exploited after the Civil War by people from outside Arkansas. The big companies took out the bauxite and made huge profits, and all they left were big open pits in the land of Arkansas. I thought it was a terrible thing, a ruthless exploitation of the weak by the strong. I thought the people of Arkansas should have benefited from those resources. They should have had an opportunity to raise their standard of living.

World War II changed a lot of that. Before the war we had been subjected to the effects of discriminatory freight rates. You could ship raw material very cheaply from Arkansas to New York, but when you shipped something finished, like a desk or a stove, from the South to the Northeast, it was very costly. It was deliberately set that way. The federal Interstate Commerce Commission set the freight rates to favor the industrial Northeast, the Yankees. That's partly how New England and the East got so rich. They exploited the rest of the country. The same type of exploitation had been practiced by

154

England with respect to the American colonies, and it contributed to the making of the American Revolution.

There is a tendency in all societies for people with power to exploit whomever they can exploit—and they did this to Arkansas. Of course a state like Texas, having ports, could not be so easily exploited, because the Texans had alternatives. We didn't. After World War II, however, Arkansas began to develop its own industry. When I got to the Senate in 1945 and served on the Banking and Currency Committee, these were issues with which I was concerned. I felt strongly that Arkansas should benefit from the exploitation of its natural resources and be able to raise the standard of living of the people and create a decent educational system.

The same applies to third-world countries today. It is simply common sense—and elementary justice—for people to feel that the national resources belonging to their country should benefit the people of that country. They should be able to benefit from their own resources. We cannot expect to go around the world any longer exploiting them as was done in the past.

This sort of cold war between the poor and the rich consumer nations that we have today has always been there, but until recently the poor nations have been unable to mobilize effective power in the conflict. Except for the oil-rich countries and perhaps a few others, the only real power available to these less-developed countries is the power of their numbers, mobilized in the General Assembly of the United Nations. The power of the so-called Group of 77 is decidedly limited, and they have made little progress in their advocacy of a New International Economic Order—but at least, for the first time in history, the poor countries of the world have a voice, and it is no longer taken for granted that the powerful will control the resources of others. Still we have not reconciled ourselves

155

to how greatly attitudes and expectations have changed. We still find it hard to recognize the deep drive of smaller nations for a meaningful independence, and harder still to come to terms with their revolutions. We still to a great degree claim the right to dominate them, as in Central America—not to incorporate them into the United States, but to have extensive economic control over them.

Our outrage over the very idea of any expropriation of American business in foreign nations suggests that we are still far from appreciating the full scope of the changes that have swept the world in this century. We have a long history of such anger—as in Mexico, or Cuba. Look at Central America. It is not just a question of our ideological obsessions, though these are central. There's no doubt that our intervention in Guatemala in 1954 against President Arbenz was decisively influenced by the United Fruit Company. John Foster Dulles had his own links with them as well.

When the Mexicans, in the 1920s, expropriated our oil concession, we were furious. But we got used to it. Countries have the right to offer reasonable compensation for foreign-owned concessions. Expropriation without any payment is not just; the principle to be applied is the same principle that applies internally: under eminent domain, the government has the right to take over private property but also has to pay a reasonable sum, which is negotiated privately or in the courts.

Internationally, if a company has developed and controls the utilization of resources in another country, that country ought to have the right to take it over and pay for it. In Cuba, when the Castro government took over the sugar mills, they ought to have paid for them—but we, in turn, ought to have been willing to accept payment. It is not healthy for any country to have its main properties run by absentee ownership. In the long run it is not good leadership to allow it.

• • •

In the 1950s, the Eisenhower years, I didn't have nearly the aversion to intervention that I later developed. I opposed Eisenhower's request for authority to send troops to Lebanon in 1958, but my position was that the principle of giving advance legislative approval of whatever might happen was bad policy. I did not expect to disapprove after the fact what he did. But when they asked us to vote on the Eisenhower doctrine, as it came to be called, we simply did not know what was going to happen and what exactly the administration was planning to do, although it was assumed that Eisenhower wanted at least contingent authority in advance to send troops to Lebanon. I simply thought it was bad procedure for Congress to sign a blank check in advance and say, "Yes, this is OK." Then we would have agreed in advance to whatever might happen and there would be no place left for advice. It would be natural that we had no role to play after doing that.

Lyndon Johnson, then Senate majority leader, disagreed with my position. He said that Eisenhower was the president, and that if we did not support him in foreign affairs, it would weaken his position in dealing with foreign governments.

I was not sure I was right about the issue at that time. It was a relatively minor affair, a procedural matter. As a precedent, though, the principle of no blank checks with regard to military commitments made excellent sense, and I deeply regret that I did not insist upon it in connection with the Tonkin Gulf resolution in 1964. But having pressed the point and failed in 1958, you tend to say, "Well, the next time I won't do it." It mattered little in 1958; it mattered a great deal in 1964.

If I wasn't critical of certain interventionist tendencies in the fifties, I was appalled by Dulles's sanctimonious moralism. I thought he was an extreme ideologue. I thought Eisenhower was mistaken in tolerating him and giving him so much power.

157

All his talk about "liberation" as against "containment" offended me—and he didn't liberate anybody. I think his piety and self-righteousness were what was most offensive. You could call it hypocrisy. I remember one phrase he used in regard to India, that it was immoral to be neutral.

My view of Eisenhower at the time was not highly favorable. I didn't think he was serious; I thought that he was just a kind of part-time president somewhat lazy, with a weakness for corporation big shots. Most of his buddies, with whom he played golf and bridge, were presidents of big companies. I don't think Ike was essentially an intellectual by nature. He was conventional and he liked power. He liked to be comfortable and he was especially comfortable with the power structure of the United States. Dulles knew how to flatter him; he was efficiently deferential. Dulles was also a lawyer for the big corporations, and that apparently added to his credentials as far as Eisenhower was concerned, because that was the power structure in the United States—the Establishment, then as it is today.

In recent years I have felt obligated to revise my assessment of Eisenhower. The contrast between what he did—and did not do—and what has happened since has elevated his reputation in my eyes. He avoided deep involvement in Vietnam. I didn't appreciate the significance of that at the time. It was only after we were deeply involved in the war that I began to realize that Eisenhower had shown commendably sound judgment in not going in as the French were losing Dien Bien Phu in 1954. On the other hand, one could criticize him, even now, and I still could, on the grounds that he should have been even more restrained and refused to send those first few hundred advisers into Vietnam, because it did open the door. I think it quite possible that if Eisenhower had said we would support the

Geneva accords, and if he had restrained Dulles from trying to upset them by immediately creating SEATO as well as by other means, the whole world might have been different.

At the time I was very uneasy with Dulles's tendency to see the Soviet Union behind every situation when something went wrong—whether it was China or Cuba. It was a perfect formula for evading reality. As a nation we seemed increasingly to be standing in the way of revolutionary change at the very time the world was in a ferment of cataclysmic change. I thought our failure in China was due to the fact that we backed the status quo through our involvement with Chiang and the nationalists. I consider the destruction of the careers of the China specialists a great loss—that generation, including John S. Service, John Paton Davis, and several other gifted analysts who were ruined by our mistaken policy on China, the demagoguery of McCarthy, and the misguided moralism of Dulles.

It is a pattern we seem bent on repeating. When people try to assert their rights against an intolerable status quo, the United States on all too many occasions sides with those who wish to retain the status quo. We align ourselves against those who would strike at corruption and tyranny, on the side of the traditional elites and the militarists who have kept their people in line.

For years, we have given money and arms willingly and unquestioningly to those governments that professed their anticommunism, however valid the disenchantment of the people might be with these regimes. And when governments refused to parrot an anticommunist line, we could not bring ourselves to assist them. Most of our aid went to the military establishments of poorer countries. We gave them on a grandiose scale the weapons of destructive warfare, at the same time that we were miserly in our aid to meaningful programs to deal with poverty. I never thought it very plausible that revolutionary change could come without revolution—peaceful or otherwise. That we, a nation born in revolution—albeit a somewhat conservative revolution—are so afraid of it that we see communists everywhere capable of dominating it, or that we have to oppose it because communists are involved, seemed pretty unconvincing to me even during the Eisenhower years.

Nonetheless, the consequences of our global interventionism were not a major concern for me in the 1950s, when I was chairing the Banking and Currency Committee. It was not until 1959, when I became chairman of the Foreign Relations Committee, that some of these issues grew more sharply etched in my mind.

Looking back at the early 1960s, I think we misread what Khrushchev was about. The anticommunist rhetoric in Kennedy's speeches then was quite vehement. I don't say this too critically: they represented an assessment of communist intentions that most of us shared at the time. But there was a prevailing conviction that, just as we had taught Stalin that "direct" aggression would not work, so must we teach Khrushchev that "indirect" aggression through wars of national liberation would not pay. Kennedy had said in his first State of the Union message that neither Russia nor China "has yielded its ambitions for world domination—ambitions which they forcefully restated only a short time ago."

Every administration since Roosevelt's has held such assumptions, an assessment that all the think tanks and most academics in the universities rarely brought up for critical examination. We acquiesced very nearly unquestioningly in the theme that was most familiar to us—the belief in the communist drive for world domination. In amplified form during Johnson's presidency, it became the basic rationale for our role in Vietnam, where we undertook to prove, once and for all, that wars of national liberation would not pay.

Looking back now, it is simply incredible what fantasies we

engaged in. The theory that Russia was the orchestrator and mentor of the international communist conspiracy, and that it was actively engaged in taking over Southeast Asia, always seemed a bit far-fetched to me. I never did find the domino theory persuasive, either. In the first place, the conflict in Vietnam was an indigenous revolution against a colonial power, France. And the Vietnamese nationalists turned to whoever could assist them, just as Castro did—or as the Nicaraguan Sandinistas do today. When we are their enemy, they have no other place to go. Notwithstanding their own adherence to communism, I think it would have been relatively easy for us to have won the friendship of the Chinese as well as the Vietnamese if we had accepted the legitimacy of their revolutions. We didn't do that; we don't accept the legitimacy of the revolution in Nicaragua today. We are paying for this attitude once again in Central America.

Indeed, I think the cold war, since Stalin's death, has been largely a misunderstanding of Russia's and China's intentions. Certainly we were given a lot of misinformation about the war in Vietnam, its justification. It was intended to stop aggression by China. That was surely, as subsequent events have shown, a misconception of China's intentions. I doubt that the Chinese have ever intended, then or now, physically to invade Southeast Asia, however much they may expect to restore their preeminent position as a political and cultural leader in that area.

Obsessive anticommunism has impaired our ability to understand modern third-world revolutions. In addition, notwithstanding our own revolutionary heritage, we are simply not a revolutionary society. We lack any experience of social revolution. As a consequence, it is practically impossible for us to have any empathy for revolutionary movements. Yet we pay ritual homage in our Fourth of July speeches, declaring that ours was indeed the "true" revolution, and an appropriate model for other countries in upheaval. Why it is so difficult to acknowledge candidly that we are not in fact "revolutionary" eludes me. Revolution is not a blessing, but a sign of social and political failure. Our lack of empathy is in this sense a byproduct of our historical good fortune and wealth. But it is intellectually and politically disabling as we try to cope with a world in which revolution is endemic and likely to remain so.

True revolutions are almost always violent—sometimes extremely so. There is not much we can do, usually, to moderate them. They are a shattering of the old social fabric and an attempt, often unsuccessful, to create alternative social values and institutions.

But revolutions in these little countries rarely if ever present any real threat to us. The only possible reason for us to get involved is overt and really serious Soviet intervention or, for that matter, intervention by anyone else. We have to recognize that these upheavals are, in many instances, authentic efforts by members of a society to internally improve their lot, to overcome the terrible inequalities of wealth and power.

It is this simple proposition that we have so much trouble accepting, because of our own unrevolutionary heritage, and because, early on in the cold war, we were sold on the idea that the Russians are behind all revolutionary movements—or will take advantage of them and turn them to their own nefarious uses. Every time there has been a revolution in Latin America—not a routine military coup, but a real revolution—we have rushed to conclude that it was communist, and if not Soviet-dominated, at least a ready avenue for Soviet exploitation. We rushed to that judgment erroneously in the Dominican Republic in 1965. And there, as in Nicaragua, I am impressed by our own historical responsibility. We were responsible for Trujillo in the Dominican Republic and for the Somoza family in Nicaragua, having trained and supported them. We had aligned ourselves with their brutal regimes and sustained them in power until their own people rose decisively against them.

It is one thing to argue—as we usually do—that we have to intervene to save American lives. I would not oppose that, and never have; but we can get our people out of these countries quickly, and then let the countries solve their own problems. Instead, we have taken the alleged urgency of protecting our own people and used it as a pretext to send in our troops—and there they remain, for quite other purposes.

As history has abundantly demonstrated, we are neither able nor much inclined to install the best people, nor to create honest, stable, democratic governments in the countries in which we intervene. It is a very difficult thing to do. We have difficulty enough with that task at home; why should we think we can do it in Nicaragua, or Grenada, or Iran, or Guatemala? It is a little like the old missionary impulse: if we can't solve our own problems, we'll go abroad and solve someone else's. The impulse is not special to us. Under the Russian tsars, when the pan-Slav ideologues found they could not do anything about their own liberties at home, they became impassioned defenders of the liberties of the Slavs outside of Russia.

I was always uneasy about our policy toward Castro. Castro had come to the United States in 1959 and had come up to the Congress, including the Senate Foreign Relations Committee, where we saw him with some of his bodyguards. It is my strong impression that when he got rid of Batista, he was widely supported. I don't myself know even today whether he was really inspired by communism in the initial stages, or whether he resorted to communism because of the hostile reaction in this country.

Cuba was an issue in the presidential campaign of 1960. Kennedy was very blunt about the perceived menace, and rumors about what was likely to happen began soon after he took office. The stories were vague; there was nothing specific

163

beyond hints and rumors about mounting an operation to oust Castro and take back Cuba.

Around Eastertime in the spring of sixty-one I had been talking with Kennedy about other matters. He asked me where I was going for Easter. I said Betty and I were going down to see her aunt in Delray, Florida, about ten miles south of Palm Beach. And he said, off the cuff, "Well I'm going down there to stay with my father. How about coming with me on the plane?"

Of course, I was very pleased to do that. So when I got back to my office and thought about it, I thought it might be a good opportunity to talk about what we had been hearing regarding a possible invasion of Cuba.

I talked to Pat Holt of the Foreign Relations Committee staff, who followed Latin American affairs, and told him about the opportunity, and so we drafted a memorandum opposing an invasion. On the plane, the president and I, and some of his staff, got to discussing Cuba. I told him that I thought it would be a mistake if an invasion was being planned. I think they acknowledged that this was coming, that this was a real possibility. I had read the stories about the training of some of the troops in Guatemala, so, since the subject had come up, I gave Kennedy my memorandum, told him I thought it would be a mistake for the reasons I outlined. I expressed doubts about the composition of the Cuban opposition, about the association of many of them with the old Batista regime, and about the lack of any realistic alternative to Castro. If the opposition won, it would inherit a country virtually bankrupt, in a state of social disorder after Castro was overthrown. And Cuba would then become our responsibility—one we should not want, and for which the risks of failure were high. I also thought that Castro had considerable popular support, that the question would consequently arise as to whether the United States should be willing to let the enterprise fail or

164

respond with the ultimate use of its own armed forces. If it came to that, we would be undoing thirty years of work in trying to live down our previous record of interventionism. Even covert support of the invasion was a violation of the spirit, if not the letter, of the law of our inter-American treaties, to say nothing of the U.N. Charter.

Kennedy listened to what I said. But he didn't say what he thought. So I left him the memo to read. Well, anyway, when it came time to return to Washington from the holiday, I got a telephone call. Kennedy hadn't said anything earlier about coming back with him, but now he asked, would I fly back with him? Of course I did.

And on the plane he said that he was going to have a press conference at the State Department and a meeting afterwards with the executive-branch leadership—not the congressional leadership. I was to be the only congressman present. After the news conference we went over to the gathering on the seventh floor of the State Department. There were the Joint Chiefs; Richard Bissell and Allen Dulles of the CIA; two or three people involved in Latin American affairs from the State Department—about ten or twelve people in all.

The question of invading Cuba was brought up. Bissell outlined the reasons and did most of the talking. He had evidently been the originator or chief advocate of the plan, which he described in detail. All this has since become public knowledge—about how they believed that with a landing of the exiles there would be a popular rising; that these fifteen hundred exiles were highly trained and that they had been organized in the last years of the Eisenhower administration. They had already spent about $40 million training these Cuban émigrés, who, if we did not proceed—so the argument went—would become a dangerous and disruptive element in all Central America. If they didn't use them for the invasion, they didn't know what else to do with them.

165

Well, they had all sorts of reasons for justifying the invasion. The most far-fetched to me was the idea that there would be an uprising if landings were made. Then Kennedy called on various people present around the table to say what they thought about it. The Joint Chiefs said it wasn't their project; it was the CIA's. But if the factors that the CIA cited about the sentiment in Cuba and all that were correct, then the chiefs thought it could probably succeed. But they were lukewarm about the whole project, I thought.

The CIA people, on the other hand, were very enthusiastic. So were several others. I recall that, beyond spelling out what was in the memorandum I had given Kennedy, I raised the question: If you succeed, what are you going to do with Cuba? We had it once and we let it go. What's the point? Well, the whole point—so they argued—was to get rid of what they called communist Castro. It wasn't in order to take over Cuba. We would install a better man. I thought that was unlikely. I didn't think it was feasible and said so.

I was a spoilsport. That was that. I just didn't think it was our business to interfere with these countries that have revolutions, trying to modernize or to escape the old feudal systems of exploitation.

I don't think my support for an invasion of Cuba in 1962 at the time of the missile crisis was inconsistent. Senator Russell and a number of us were called by the White House at five o'clock on the day President Kennedy was to make the announcement of his planned actions at seven, and we were told the alternatives that had been considered were an embargo, a quarantine, and an invasion. Senator Russell and I were both of the view that an invasion of Cuba would be less provocative of the Soviet Union than confronting their ships on the high seas, since Cuba was not Soviet territory and an American landing would allow the Russians to stand aside while we dealt with the Cubans.

What was proposed was that if the Soviet ships did not turn back after our warning, we would take them or sink them. We did not know about the letters exchanged between Kennedy and Khrushchev. Neither Senator Russell nor I had been consulted that day until five. The Soviet ships were on the high seas, where they had a right to be. To sink a Soviet ship would have been a direct, flagrant act of war. We weren't at war with Cuba. We had no legitimate right, in terms of international law, to impose an embargo or a quarantine. But the president had already made up his mind. He had not brought in the congressional leadership for consultation, although that was not at first clear to us. He just wanted, as a courtesy, to bring us in for a briefing before leaving the meeting to make a speech announcing the embargo.

With the possible exception of Cuba in 1962, because of the Soviet missiles, I don't think there is a single Latin American country where we had valid reason to intervene over the years since World War II. Except for going in and getting our citizens out if they are endangered, we should not be involved in opposing an indigenous revolution. We have neither interests of our own nor the capacity to be helpful that might justify our large-scale involvement or spending a lot of money in such countries as Angola, Ethiopia, or Nicaragua. We should not be supplying arms, either to the governments of these countries or to those who are fighting against them, so that we end up aligned with forces engaged in bitter internal conflicts.

We should intervene *only* when—and without any question—our own real interests are threatened. I don't know how to make this assertion strong enough—other than to say that we ought not to intervene unless a truly vital national interest

167

is at stake. For example, and quite obviously, it is crucial to us that the Soviet Union not overcome, by force, western Europe. I don't think they are going to try. It would be madness, and they are not mad. But it is a matter of vital interest, as is Japan, because here we get into areas where the fundamental balance of power might be seriously upset. Otherwise I have difficulty thinking of a case of justified intervention. But possible military threats to our allies go beyond the question of revolution. These are matters of overt aggression. That is not the kind of circumstance we encountered in Vietnam or encounter in Central America today.

Our military involvement in Nicaragua, through surrogates, has been a serious mistake—just as Vietnam was. The Sandinistas are not a threat to us. There is little persuasive evidence that the Soviets have at any time made a major effort in aiding them. They have encouraged them, to be sure, backing them with small amounts of arms and large amounts of rhetoric—an essentially limited effort calculated to irritate us. That is the game. We do the same to them when the opportunity arises.

The only possible justification for our intervention in Nicaragua would be overt and serious intervention by the Soviets, or perhaps Cuba with Soviet support, that could prevent the local people from determining their own future, or mounting their own revolution. But even this is a slippery criterion; there are always people around, on both sides of an issue, who are getting involved—directly and indirectly. Overall I don't believe the Russians have taken a very large role in Central America and Nicaragua. At least since the time of the Cuban missile crisis, they have recognized the region as an American sphere of influence, just as we have recognized eastern Europe as a Soviet sphere of influence, little as each of us has cared to acknowledge it.

We are inclined to overlook the appalling conditions that

fuel these revolutions. And we seem at times to be oblivious of the practical restraints on our power.

The charge is sometimes made, as it was in the days of Vietnam, that nonintervention reflects indifference, as if the worst thing we Americans can do to anybody is to leave them alone. The question—or accusation—is then put: Aren't they—the Nicaraguans or Salvadorans—entitled to some consideration? Don't they deserve freedom and a taste of the good life?

Lyndon Johnson, Hubert Humphrey, and others used to say that I was a racist, and that was why I didn't like the war in Vietnam. I didn't think "the little brown people" were entitled to democracy. "We want to bring them the Great Society," Hubert would say. "We're not racists. We have a great interest in those brown people." And all the time bombing them from five miles up. Yet they'd say of me, "He's always been a racist. He's from the South."

This view that the world can be easily shaped and dominated by the great powers is a source of endless folly, for us and for the Russians. Small countries wish to find their own way, make their own mistakes. Neither the Russians nor we can easily dominate others. I don't know what the Russians will do in eastern Europe; they have a complicated, difficult situation on their hands. What happened to them in Egypt—from which they were unceremoniously expelled—is likely to happen elsewhere, as long as we are not there to push the people concerned into the continued embrace of the Russians. These countries don't like to throw off one yoke in order to take on another. I can't believe that the peoples of Angola and Mozambique who rejected the Portuguese are going to turn around and become subservient to Russia. In their poverty and great need, they accept aid and advisers, of course. So did we accept aid from abroad, during our revolution, from the French. It may look temporarily like subservience, but in the long run, I don't think you'll see the out-side power in charge.

While our overt interventions have gained us little, our covert interventions have gained us less. The gradual development of the CIA as an operator in the field and all of its various covert operations have been on the whole a disservice to the country. The Iran-contra affair is only the latest in a long series of fiascos. I cannot think of a single covert operation of this kind that was necessary or in the long run really successful.

They used to boast about displacing the nationalist Mossadeq and restoring the shah to power in 1953. I think that proved to be a great mistake. By the time Carter faced the problem, there wasn't much he could do about Iran. The pressures had been building up for over twenty years. We started there in 1953 by restoring the shah and supplying him with arms without much attention to the real needs of the people. It culminated in the explosion that drove the shah from power and installed the radical fundamentalist regime of Khomeini. Looking back on these events and our involvement in them, it is now clear that our intervention in 1953 was unwise. The reason is that it takes time for reactions to set in, and we are just not smart enough to tamper with such things. No one is. Then when the explosion comes and you get a Khomeini, it becomes almost impossible for Americans to think seriously about what really happened. Outraged as we inevitably were by the seizure of our hostages, we were in no mood to reflect on the possibility that our intervention and subsequent support of the shah had perhaps not been such a good idea, or the possibility that our idea of a good society did not appeal to the Iranian people. When Khomeini and these people suggest that our concept of a good society doesn't suit them, it shocks us, and we can't help but think it's all stirred up by the Russians or that it's some form of madness.

Nobody knows what would have happened if we had stayed out of Iran in the 1950s, but in all likelihood the worst thing would probably have been the expropriation of the oil companies largely owned by the British.

Our intervention in Guatemala in 1954 was a mistake for much the same reason. You must think of these things in the long haul. What looks like a quick success turns into a slow-motion disaster. Neither we nor anybody else to my knowledge have the kind of wisdom that would enable us to intervene forcibly and shape the policies of others. We have all we can do and more, it would seem, to cope with our own problems; to suppose that we alone can help guide the intricate internal affairs of other nations is folly. If there is a way to bring influence to bear, it is by example—the example of intelligent management of our own affairs.

It is easy to say—and often is said—that we cannot have tolerable relations with new revolutionary regimes. The problem is that our anticommunist paranoia has made it impossible to find out. We do not know whether Mao's declared interest in a relationship with the Americans in the 1940s or Ho Chi Minh's were sincere. And the reason we don't know is that we never tried to find out. Those who reported it was a possibility were hounded out of the foreign service because of our suspicion and fear of communism. The legacy of that era brings to mind Ivan the Terrible's practice of murdering the bearer of bad news. We are more civilized than that; we have been content simply to ruin people's careers.

If we were not so hostile to revolutionary regimes such as the Sandinistas, they would in all likelihood gradually forsake Marxism and revert to traditional social and economic prac-

171

tices simply because they work better and are more productive. If they have the choice, and are not under outside pressure, they will try to experiment with other ways of organizing their societies. That's what the Chinese are doing today. And so is Gorbachev. Without the pressures of the arms race, the cold war, and our unrelenting hostility, I think you would see similar forces at work in the self-declared Marxist regimes of the third world.

It is understandably difficult, for example, to get off to a good start with a new revolutionary regime when you plot to kill its leaders. If we start to plan to assassinate leaders we don't like, as the CIA is believed to have done with Castro, you are only asking for trouble. It's self-defeating. It is against our interests. I don't think it ever succeeds. It gives others an excuse to engage in terrorism, to kill our ambassadors or citizens traveling aboard. You start a process of terrorism that has far-reaching and unpredictable consequences. There is a good case to be made that we initiated it. We and some of our friends have initiated some of the worst aspects of modern terrorism.

I am not against foreign aid. The annual foreign aid authorization bill was under the jurisdiction of the Senate Foreign Relations Committee, and for years after 1959, when I became chairman of the committee, I served as sponsor and floor manager of that legislation in the Senate. I was, however, always more comfortable with the idea of multinational channels of providing aid, and late in my career I began to oppose direct bilateral aid. The early Point Four program of the 1940s was a good model for the encouragement of self-help, but we moved away from that concept with grievous consequences. Point Four was comparable to the old agricultural extension services in this country, under which we helped farmers with

172

new methods of agriculture, to guide them away from the old one-crop system in the South, for example. I thought from the beginning that there were great risks in moving towards military aid, that this was the wrong approach. Bilateral aid was too easily distorted into a means of exerting the wrong kind of political pressure; if we were serious about economic development, it seemed to me that it should be internationalized. When the aid is bilateral, the temptation is all but irresistible to put it to political use—to win votes in the United Nations, or to win marketable gratitude, or to gain a compliant surrogate. Under the pressure of such temptations we were too willing to build a flashy steel plant for a developing country when what it really needed was improved agricultural methods. Or sometimes we just gave them food rather than help them make their own agricultural economics viable.

Although assistance through international agencies, including the United Nations, is derided, I remain convinced that this is the only promising avenue for effective long-term assistance to the third world. A foreign-aid program tied to narrow national interest and national power is not going to work in the long run; it is not working now.

From the start, however, instead of using the United Nations, we sought to gain political influence through aid. That approach has been shown to be inefficient, from the standpoint of both influence for the donor and development for the recipient. Our bilateral programs were fraught with serious weaknesses. We should long ago have internationalized economic aid and extended it exclusively through the United Nations agencies and the World Bank, to dissociate it from political interference. It is still, in my judgment, a sound idea—the one form of "intervention" that makes political and economic sense.

6

THE
MIDDLE EAST

The only long-term alternative to endless warfare in the Middle East is a general settlement. I have thought ever since the 1956 Suez War that the best way to settle the situation was to do what Eisenhower did at that time—require Israel to return to its original borders. In return, as I first proposed in 1970, I would extend to Israel binding guarantees in the form of a security treaty as well as multilateral guarantees through the United Nations. But from the outset I underestimated the depth of Israel's fear and mistrust and its consequent determination to retain the Arab-populated territories seized in 1967.

I had hoped that Israel, because of its technological talents and its highly literate population, could be a workshop—a technological and intellectual center for the Middle East. It would be beneficial to the Arab countries; they could gain a wide range of advantages in development from economic ties to Israel. It would be mutually beneficial.

This, as I understand it, was the hope of Nahum Goldmann, the late president of the World Jewish Congress. It was a theory that greatly influenced me. Goldmann had raised the question whether an Israel armed to the teeth and constantly at war could fulfill its Zionist ideal of a homeland for Jewish culture and religion. He wanted Israel to become the Switzerland of the Middle East, with its borders guaranteed by the nations of the world, including its Arab neighbors. And he was deeply concerned that in the long run the balance of power would shift towards the Arabs with their oil resources, their greater numbers, and their increasing technological capacity.

The government of Israel never took kindly to these suggestions, although Goldmann was one of the major contributors to the founding of Israel. And they surely haven't taken to my ideas, either, which were influenced by Goldmann's.

Today, after decades of conflict, all of the most difficult issues remain—focused on the West Bank, Gaza, and Jerusalem. As demonstrated by the recent and continuing *intifadeh*—or uprising—on the part of the Palestinians under occupation, there will be war, and more war, until the basic issues are resolved. Israel has the upper hand now, but at the price of being a garrison state; and there is no guarantee that some future war will not eventually devastate Israel.

It is up to us in collaboration with the Soviet Union and the United Nations to prevent that. Israel has been stalling—and, under its present government, seems to have nothing more concrete in mind than getting all the arms and money it can from the U.S. The costs of this stalling, the creation of a garrison state in Israel, are manifested in the *intifadeh.* Israel's leaders might have made good use of time that has now passed to prepare for the necessary accommodations. They might have been telling their people, as David Ben-Gurion tried to tell them in 1971, that peace is Israel's "great necessity," and "to get it we must return to the borders before 1967."

Ben-Gurion, whom I met in Israel in 1959, was a clever and intelligent man. While in office he was quite aggressive, however, and only later did he argue that there could be no real security unless there were peaceful borders and friendly neighbors. That happens so often—that people, when they are in responsible positions, cater to the popular attitudes that are so often chauvinistic. Only in retirement did Ben-Gurion become a more objective statesman, but by then he could do little. The same is true of our leaders: had Presidents Ford and Carter been as forthright on the Palestinian issue while they were in office as they have been since leaving office, significant progress towards a settlement might have been made.

Israel confronts a virtually inevitable shift in the balance of power in the Middle East. This prospective shift is more than a matter of weapons and fighting skills. The rise of the Arabs and the Palestinians is based upon two powerful and growing forces—enormous wealth that comes through oil, and the surging nationalism of the Arabs, especially the embittered, tenacious nationalism of the Palestinians. The spectacular but probably transient ascendancy of the Israelis has been based primarily on human assets—discipline, energy, bravery, and competence. Impressive as these qualities are, Israel is still a small country with modest natural resources and heavy liabilities—with no oil, with an economy burdened by military costs and inflation, an economy so dependent on the United States as to make Israel—however little we or the Israelis care to admit it—a client state of the United States.

The friends of Israel in the United States do her no service by refusing to recognize these facts of power and change. Perhaps a siege mentality among Israelis is understandable; but it is much less so among their supporters in this country, who, by underwriting intransigence, have long encouraged Israel on a course that may lead to her destruction, and possibly—given the real possibilities of escalation—to ours as well.

The Israelis and their supporters here—especially the latter—have long taken the position that if you do not do exactly as they wish, you are anti-Israel and antisemitic. Accordingly, since no one welcomes these charges and the political sanctions that go with them, it has been impossible to follow what I would call an evenhanded policy in the Middle East. It has not been possible in the past; and it still isn't. Any member of

Congress who does not follow the wishes of the Israel lobby is bitterly denounced and can be assured of finding his opponent richly funded in the next election.

The Israelis have been critical of me going back at least to the time of the 1956 war. I had strongly supported the building of the Aswan Dam in Egypt. As the chairman at that time of the Banking and Currency Committee, I had become well acquainted with Eugene Black, who was president of the World Bank. We became good friends, our friendship having grown out of the fact that the postwar Bretton Woods agreement related to banking and currency, and that the American role in the World Bank's business was under the jurisdiction of the Banking and Currency Committee. Black had advised me about the Aswan Dam. The project had originated with the World Bank, which was putting up much of the money and designing the plans. It was a good program.

When John Foster Dulles abruptly canceled our involvement and withdrew the offer to help the Egyptians, I was extremely put out. His moralism, the way he approached subjects—a kind of holier-than-thou view that it was immoral to be neutral and all that sort of thing—had irritated me very much. The Egyptians had been stalling and putting off a final decision, but they had finally made up their minds that they would accept the project. That was the day Dulles withdrew the offer—objecting, among other things, to the Egyptians' developing relations with the Chinese. Dulles was extremely chauvinistic and narrow-minded with regard to the Chinese; his view was that it was a mortal sin for the Egyptians or anyone else even to communicate with them, or to consider getting arms from them or from any eastern European nation.

We conducted a study of the affair, but the Foreign Relations Committee couldn't agree. It was split on partisan lines. Another contentious issue arose when Senator Paul Douglas of Illinois offered an amendment to the aid bill, providing for sanctions designed to force the Egyptians to allow Israeli ships through the Suez Canal. I objected to the amendment on the ground that this was a misuse of the aid bill. I thought the Egyptians ought to allow the Israelis free passage, in accordance with general international law such as applied to the Turkish straits. I just didn't think it was proper to put that provision in an aid bill. To use aid as a political weapon in forcing countries to do things that they did not want to do, I thought, distorted the whole theory of aid. That's not aid. That's a system of bribery or blackmail. I am not opposed to—in fact I favor—withholding bilateral aid from countries committed to using that aid for purposes detrimental to the national interests of the United States, but using aid as an instrument of coercion in matters involving the recipient's relations with third countries is quite another matter.

In any event, I was criticized. The Israelis didn't like my attitude. They wanted to use any available means—at their own disposal or ours—to advance their national purposes. In the spring of 1959 I went to Egypt and Israel. I visited with President Nasser in a modest cottage, on the edge of Cairo. I found him to be an attractive man, without pretense, and he expressed a clear desire to develop good relations with us. He complained about some speeches in the Congress and particularly about certain articles in the *New York Times*. He apparently read the *Times* carefully and felt that it never gave his point of view accurately and never gave the Egyptian point of view a fair shake. The editors of the *Times*, by Nasser's reckoning, were completely devoted to the Israeli government's point of view. That was one reason, I think, why he said that I was one of the few people in the Congress who seemed to understand Egyptian and Arab viewpoints and was interested in what later came to be called an evenhanded policy.

My reception in Israel was quite different. I had been invited to lecture at Tel Aviv University. When I arrived there the students picketed me with umbrellas, the implication being that I had performed like Neville Chamberlain at Munich in giving way to the Egyptians, particularly in connection with my opposition to the Douglas amendment to the aid bill. That had caused considerable resentment in Israel. Anyway, they picketed and made it impossible for me to deliver the lecture. I got up on the podium and it was clear that the students were determined to disrupt the meeting and prevent me from being heard. So the lecture was not delivered.

The speech was not to have been anti-Israel. I was trying to be pro-American—that is, to suggest policies that would serve our interests and bring peace in the area between the Egyptians and the Israelis. Many people then thought it was possible to bring about some peaceful settlement. There were various proposals under consideration for such projects as the cooperative development of irrigation and water supply on some of the rivers. I'd seen a lot of impressive development in agriculture; they were putting their aid to good use in such areas. And the armosphere was not nearly as tense as it is now.

So completely have many of our principal officeholders fallen under Israeli influence that they not only deny today the legitimacy of Palestinian national aspirations, but debate who more passionately opposes a Palestinian state. Eisenhower was the last president to stand up to the Israelis—at a time when the Israel lobby was not nearly as well organized and as well funded as it is today. In 1956, when the Israelis, along with the French and the British, invaded Egypt, he insisted that they withdraw. He threatened to support sanctions in the United Nations and also to challenge the tax-exempt status of private contributions to Israel. In effect, he said, "If you don't withdraw we'll cut off your money." He demonstrated, at least at that time, that you could oppose them. But, as a consequence of this, supporters of Israel mobilized to create the powerful Israel lobby that exists in this nation today. Under the direction of B'nai B'rith and many other organizations, they have created the most effective political lobbying group in the United States. The only influence that can compete with them in a real contest is the Pentagon, which, with its allies in the military-industrial complex, can muster as many votes in the Congress as the Israelis can. The only contests the Israelis have lost since that time were over the sale of F-15 fighter planes to Saudi Arabia in 1978 and the sale of AWACs to Saudi Arabia in 1981. The Pentagon was of course involved in the case of the AWACs, and there were also $18 billion of cash payments involved—which were too persuasive. And so the Pentagon prevailed, but only after bitter and protracted debates and by narrow votes in the Senate. The lobby can just about tell the President what to do when it comes to Israel. Its influence in Congress is pervasive and, I think, profoundly harmful—to us and ultimately to Israel itself.

For many years I have felt that the situation in the Middle East was very nearly hopeless. The fundamental problem for us is that we have lost our freedom of action in the Middle East and are committed to policies that promote neither our own national interest nor the cause of peace. AIPAC (the American-Israel Public Affairs Committee) and its allied organizations have effective working control of the electoral process. They can elect or defeat nearly any congressman or senator that they wish, with their money and coordinated organizations. They are the really important power to negotiate with in the Middle East if you want an agreement. If you want to sell arms to Saudi Arabia, it is necessary to confront them. If you want to sell arms to Jordan, you need their permission. If you wish to cooperate with the Soviet Union to bring about a peaceful settlement, you must, because of the power of their lobby, first obtain Israel's permission.

In short, the Israeli government dominates our policy in the Middle East. It does so in part because its influence grows out of our rivalry with the Russians. They have convinced Americans that they are the main bulwark against Soviet expansion in the Middle East. That is a very dubious proposition, but they have sold it to the American public; they believe it and so do the Americans.

Over the years, we have nearly allowed our policy of détente to go on the rocks over the issue of Jewish emigration from the Soviet Union—a matter of limited relevance to the basic issue of human rights in the Soviet Union and of even less relevance to the vital interests of the United States. When Senator Jackson invoked Article 13 of the Universal Declaration of Human Rights selectively in support of Jewish emigration, he effectively obfuscated the matter. Article 13 states, "Everyone has the right to leave any country, including his own, and to return to his country." Note that the article refers not only to the right to leave but also to the right to return. Is the right of the Palestinians to return to the homes from which they were expelled any less fundamental than the right of Soviet Jews to make new homes in a new land?

Perhaps this will change as Gorbachev demonstrates a more conciliatory Soviet attitude not only on Jewish emigration but on the terms of a possible general settlement of the Israeli-Palestinian conflict. For my part I welcome these Soviet initiatives, not only as a means of advancing a settlement in the Middle East but as a means too of removing a powerful obstacle to détente.

All this points to what has long been a fundamental problem in our policy—our loss of any genuine freedom of action in the Middle East. Some members of Congress are quite ardent in their support of Israel; others are simply politically intimidated. It's often a combination. Nobody likes to talk about these matters, even in private. I think some of my colleagues felt I was being foolish to raise issues about Israel and the Middle East at all. I thought I was being evenhanded, that we should treat the Arabs and Israel with respect and try to reconcile their differences. But this did not satisfy the Israelis.

In recent years, there has been more dissent in Israel, certainly more than in this country. For an Israeli to raise questions with the Knesset or the press is more or less acceptable, but for an American official or representative to raise questions here is to incur harsh and swift political retribution.

Israel can and should survive as a peaceful, prosperous society—but within the essential borders of 1967 as called for by the Security Council's Resolution 242 of November 1967. That resolution called for the guarantee of the territorial inviolability and political independence of every state in the area, as well as for the inadmissibility of the acquisition of territory by force. As I have suggested on numerous occasions going back to 1970, this can be implemented through great-power guarantees contracted through the United Nations Security Council, and in addition, by an explicit, binding American treaty guarantee of Israel.

That much we owe them, but no more. We do not owe them our support of their continued occupation of Arab lands, including old Jerusalem and the Palestinian West Bank and Gaza. The Palestinian people have as much right to a homeland as do the Jewish people. We Americans, who have always professed adherence to the principle of self-determination, should be the first to appreciate that. The main requirement of a settlement is that it accord a reasonably secure national existence to both Israelis and Palestinians, and that can only mean the partition of old Palestine along the approximate borders of 1967. Of all the peoples in the area, the Palestinians have been dealt the greatest injustice. Correcting that injustice, to the extent that it can be corrected, is the central requirement for peace in that area.

The general outlines for a peace are there: explicit acknowledgement of Israel's right to exist by the Arabs, including the

Palestinians; Israeli withdrawal to the approximate borders of 1967, with United Nations forces patrolling demilitarized zones on both sides of Israel's borders; self-determination for the Palestinian people, with the Israelis accepting the Palestinians, represented by the PLO, as negotiating partners with a right to form a state of their own; a special status for the old city of Jerusalem providing equal and uninhibited access for members of all faiths; and a general great-power guarantee of the settlement and its terms, under the auspices of the United Nations, reinforced by direct American treaty guarantees of Israel's independence and territory. The Soviets have stated repeatedly that they would join us in sponsoring and guaranteeing a settlement along these lines, including the guarantee to Israel.

To state the situation with simple candor: The United States has done as much for Israel as one nation can do for another—we, and we alone, have made it possible for Israel to exist as a state. Surely it is not too much to ask in return that Israel give up East Jerusalem and the West Bank and Gaza, and acknowledge a Palestinian right to self-determination, as the necessary means of breaking a chain of events that threatens everyone with ultimate ruin.

For Israel to say that Jerusalem is non-negotiable is unreasonable. The original United Nations resolution of 1947 creating Israel specified that Jerusalem should have a special status. That means a status other than being part of a sovereign state. A special status means that Jerusalem should be internationalized—under the United Nations or under a joint Israeli-Palestinian jurisdiction in which the usual attributes of sovereignty of the two administering countries would be suspended.

It is difficult to generate much optimism, however. There is not much chance of getting support—or even a fair hearing—for the Palestinians in this country. Perhaps the one hope lies in making real progress with the Soviet Union. Reaching an understanding with the Russians on the Middle East would do more than practically anything else in the long run to under-cut the power of the Israel lobby—which is why they are against it. Without the ability to plead their role in opposing the Russians, I doubt that the Israelis would so easily be able to obtain the appropriations they now require to survive as a garrison state.

7

SEEING THE WORLD AS OTHERS SEE IT

When all is said and done, when the subtleties and abstractions of strategy and power have all been explained, we remain confronted with the most fundamental questions about war and peace, and why we contest the issues we do, and why we even care about them. Why, after all, is it that so much of the energy and intelligence of nations is used to make life painful and difficult for other peoples and nations, rather than to make life better for all? Why are we willing to fight and die over ideological questions and sacrifice so much for abstractions so remote from personal satisfactions that bring fulfillment to our lives?

The conflicting beliefs and ideologies of peoples, as well as their religions, often seem purely a matter of accident as to where an individual was born. If the same people had been born somewhere else, they would have opposite beliefs. There seems to be no particular intellectual commitment in these matters. Yet the beliefs become so strong we are quite willing to fight and be killed for them. It has never made any deep human sense to me that a man or woman believes in Islam if he or she is born in an Arab country and in Christianity if he or she happens to be born in a Christian country. If we could recognize and acknowledge the importance of accidental factors in shaping our ideological beliefs, the willingness to fight and kill over them ought to cease. To take them so seriously that we are willing to destroy whole nations because of them or on behalf of them seems irrational to me.

"There may be arguments about the best way of raising wheat in a cold climate or of reforesting a denuded mountain. But such arguments never lead to organized slaughter," Aldous Huxley noted. "Organized slaughter is the result of arguments about such questions as the following: Which is the best nation? The best religion? The best political theory? The best form of government? Why are other people so stupid and wicked? Why can't they see how good and intelligent we are? Why do they resist our beneficent efforts to bring them under our control and make them like ourselves?"*

It may be very naïve to think the human race can do much about its traditions and its customs, but I am unable to accept the view that we are helpless products of our experience and conditioning. It reminds me of the argument that has gone on among anthropologists about whether or not man is instinctively, biologically, inherently aggressive. Some have argued that this tendency to attack other people is a biological compulsion. I don't find this persuasive. There are very few animals that take pleasure in killing or at least indiscriminately killing their own species. Writers such as Konrad Lorenz point out that there are only a few animals—like rats—that will kill their own species for purposes other than the protection of their territory or their mates. In certain circumstances, killing of this kind—the ethologists call it "intraspecific aggression"—is defensive. Many species kill for food, but few if any deliberately just go out and enjoy, you might say, attacking and killing other animals, of their own or other species. And they certainly don't kill other animals for ideological purposes.

Some anthropologists have advanced the view that man in the original state of nature had to be cooperative or he would

*Aldous Huxley, "The Politics of Ecology" (pamphlet, published by the Center for the Study of Democratic Institutions, Santa Barbara, Calif., 1963), p. 6.

not have survived. He could not have survived with his poor equipment, compared to other animals, and with his lack of protective covering—no thick heavy fur, no claws, no long teeth. He had to be cooperative to survive. That argument (perhaps for ideological reasons) appeals to me.

War may have had some purpose, in the old days, as a form of expression of people's interests—it was not so disastrous to society in the old days. You could even make some arguments that it contributed to progress. It loosened up some of the old rigid ways in certain societies. It is, I suppose, possible to make a case for the usefulness of war in at least some instances before the invention of weapons of mass destruction. I find it uncongenial, but I can understand the argument. But with modern weapons—and this even before nuclear weapons—war becomes so destructive that it is highly, profoundly irrational.

At the time of the invention of the atomic bomb, Einstein made his famous and perceptive statement about the essentiality for man to develop a new way of thinking about international relations, failing which, we would be faced with incalculable catastrophe. I believe that. I don't think men and women want to commit suicide. Therefore, what do we do about it? Everybody says, "Sure, we want to do something. We don't want war. We want peace. We want to find a way to peace." The difficulty is, what do you *do* about it? We have all agreed on the objective, but few can agree on what you actually do about it.

I have thought of everything I can think of, and the one thing that gives me some hope is the ethos that underlies the educational-exchange program. That ethos, in sum, is the belief that international relations can be improved, and the danger of war significantly reduced, by producing generations of leaders, especially in the big countries, who through the experience of educational exchange, will have acquired some feeling and understanding of other peoples' cultures—why they operate as they do, why they think as they do, why they react as they do—and of the differences among these cultures. It is possible—not very probable, but possible—that people can find in themselves, through intercultural education, the ways and means of living together in peace.

That same ethos is found in Freud's answer to Einstein's query in 1932 about the prospects for mankind doing anything about war. In a responding essay, Freud concluded that there was perhaps not much hope for eliminating war, but such hope as there was lay in man's capacity for cultural development, which to me is quite consistent with the idea of exchanges to promote cultural development among people of differing cultures.

The most interesting hearings I ever held in the Senate Foreign Relations Committee, in 1966 and 1969, dealt with the psychological aspects of international relations. A number of eminent psychiatrists testified on psychological insights that might be pertinent to international relations. I have always regarded those hearings as pioneering, although they were not appreciated much then or now. They came about as a result of a letter I received from Dr. Jerome Frank of Johns Hopkins University. He said that if we wanted to get along with the Russians, we should do the opposite of what we were then doing as a country; that instead of challenging them on every occasion, we should seek out ways to do things together so as gradually to ameliorate our animosity.

One of my objectives in those hearings was to encourage Americans to engage in a bit of self-examination that might lead to some changes in our conduct. Why, for example, with all of our technological capacity and our high standard of living, were we so blind, as it seemed to me, to some of our own actions—including our actions at that time in Vietnam? I was not suggesting that we were worse than others—but that as a great power we were acting all too similarly to other great powers in the past, or to put it another way, that we had made little if any progress in advancing the evolution of human relations.

Countries such as Spain in the days of Philip II, or England during the last century, or Germany just prior to World War I, were in their respective eras the most advanced country scientifically, culturally, economically. Yet, to put it mildly, their activities abroad scarcely reflected the vaunted standards of their civilizations. I saw us acting in the same pattern that had been followed by our predecessors, and doing so with nuclear weapons that could lead, in the end, only to catastrophe. We had to break the pattern—to begin to do something never before accomplished. That, or something like it, was the goal towards which we groped in those hearings on the psychological aspects of international relations.

It was not a question of our good intentions. Countries that achieve great power have long had a tendency to identify themselves with the deity or with high standards of virtue, and, on the basis of this identification, to develop a form of messianism, a conviction that it is their duty to take their message to other people. We might be doing this, with the best of intentions, but the result was a pattern of intervention in one way or another throughout the globe—militarily, politically, or economically. Are such motives, such high estimations of one's own country, necessarily a characteristic of a powerful society? Is there a compulsion of such great powers to believe that they are better than anyone else and thus have a duty to proselytize? Are they bound to take the view that they are the chosen people who are responsible for spreading the gospel?

If we could understand the forces and factors that shape our beliefs, we might learn how to alter our conduct. If we could focus on the passions engendered by our belief in abstractions

195

associated with the nation-state, we might better understand the limits of our own ideological view of the world, and learn the necessity for understanding how much we need to view others through *their* perceptions, assumptions, beliefs.

If we could understand these differences, we might in the process acquire some capacity for empathy. Our capacity for decent behavior seems to vary directly with our perception of others as individual humans with human motives and feelings, whereas man's capacity for barbaric acts seems to increase with the perception of adversaries in abstract terms. It is the only explanation that makes some sense of how some good and decent Americans who might reach out to their neighbors to help cope with someone's personal illness or misfortune could speak of the Russians as beyond the pale of humanity, or could celebrate the number of Viet Cong killed in a week, or—in the days before reconciliation—could refer to the Chinese not as people but as hordes of blue ants. It is not that we feel savage inhumanity towards those who do not share our beliefs; it is rather that we cannot quite see them as humans at all. The obvious value of liberating the imagination is that it might enable us to acquire some understanding of the worldview held by people whose past experiences and present circumstances and beliefs are radically different from our own. It might enable us, for example, to understand how people in poor or brutally misgoverned countries are driven to revolution, perhaps even to see why some of them are communists.

We might also hope, through the humanization of discourse and inquiry, to start to understand the dehumanized way we now discuss our national security—as if, in our sophisticated scenarios of nuclear war, of first strike and counterstrike, we were dealing with abstractions and not with the lives of peoples and civilizations. It is the abstractions that seem to dehumanize us. In the Vietnam years we found ourselves treating the life and death and suffering of the Vietnamese as not significant in themselves but as mere factors in strategic and political calculations. The leaders who led us into Vietnam were not monsters, but honorable, decent, often intelligent officials who nonetheless abandoned considerations of humanity at water's edge—because, I strongly suspect, the enemy had become in their minds an abstraction. And the same can be said of the gifted, personally quite decent "defense intellectuals" who become bloodless, computerized calculators when it comes to the arms race. We make policy apart from the image of what our world would be like after a war—or, as in the case of Vietnam or Nicaragua, apart from any awareness of the piles of decomposing bodies, the mutilated children, the cemeteries, and the broken lives that are always the tangible human results of any war.

It is not that we become insensate monsters when we are discussing the arms race or some regional war. It is more as though we don't really believe our own words. We are talking about things as if they were unreal. We are talking about them in the abstract; and in the abstract—megadeaths, throw weights—they *are* unreal. We are acknowledging possibilities that we do not really feel to be possibilities, because they are so far outside anything we have ever experienced. Even a word like "megadeath" has an antiseptic sound. It doesn't sound like blood and pain and burns and mutilation. Nor is there any resonance of human travail and suffering in the Pentagonese acronym for small wars in Nicaragua or Angola. These wars are LICs—"low-intensity conflicts." What does an LIC have to do with broken lives and shattered limbs?

Given all this, and despite the anesthetizing effects of the discourse of abstraction, why is it that a military, chauvinistic view often seems to appeal to the public more than a hopeful, optimistic set of ideas that might make our country and our world a better place in which to live? Is there any hope of outgrowing this preoccupation with violence, of delivering ourselves from the prospect of warfare?

We do not like to acknowledge how thin the veneer of civilization really is. We do not like to consider the possibility that this preoccupation with security may be partly understood as a heritage of our tribal past, when the risk of being destroyed could be constant and immediate; or that in foreign relations, in dealing with a foreign country, we tap into this almost tribal instinct. If you challenge the conventional details of a tax bill, or of a program to build roads, you don't unleash the kind of responses you elicit when you raise questions about foreign relations. Even the somewhat simple, unsophisticated way in which I pose the issue here is probably hard for Americans to accept or consider—unless they happen to be analysts or anthropologists.

I come back to Freud's letter to Einstein. If you want to prevent war, you have to understand how deep its roots are. The impulse to fight and kill may be ineradicably implanted in our genes, and if that is true, there would not seem to be much we can do about it. But if its roots, as Freud suggests, are cultural relics of our tribal past, then it may be we can do something about it. If we are aggressive by nature, there is nothing much to be done except to acknowledge our weakness and our consequent need for the military. But this is indeed a weakness; it is not a source of real strength. I am more inclined to—and much more comfortable with—the view that our aggressive impulses are culturally rooted, and that we can do something about them, through education and the understanding of what other countries and cultures are about. Our survival depends on this capacity for imagination and empathy, compassion and understanding of diversity. And it will, in the end, require that we succeed in transferring at least some small part of our feelings of loyalty and responsibility from the sovereign nation to some larger political community.

The primary obstacle to any meaningful progress toward that goal arises from our dealings with the Soviet Union—our obsession with it, our preoccupation with it, our willingness to bankrupt ourselves in the awful arms race. The depiction of them as evil releases some of our worst, not our best, qualities. It reminds me of Huxley's warning: "Those who crusade not for good in themselves but against the devil in others never succeed in making the world better but leave it either as it was or sometimes even perceptibly worse than it was before the crusade began. By thinking primarily of evil we tend, however excellent our intentions, to create occasions for evil to manifest itself."*

Early in my career I focused on the two areas of activity in foreign relations that I considered to be the most crucial, and also the most promising. One was the need of an international peacekeeping organization, the other the need of international education. I still believe in the United Nations—not the debilitated, often irresponsible body that sits in New York, but the concept underlying the United Nations, which cannot be said to have failed because it has never been seriously tried. It also seemed to me—and still does—that the vital mortar to seal the bricks of world order is education across international boundaries, not with the expectation that knowledge would make us love each other, but in the hope that it would encourage empathy between nations, and foster the emergence of

*Quoted in *Psychological Aspects of International Relations,* hearings before the Senate Committee on Foreign Relations, May 25, 1966 (Washington, D.C.: U.S. Government Printing Office, 1966), p. 51.

leaders whose sense of other nations and cultures would enable them to shape specific policies based on tolerance and rational restraint.

With few interruptions the trend of events since World War II had been against these concepts. Accordingly, I found myself resisting what seemed to me the excesses of the cold war, culminating in the tragic war in Vietnam and the ongoing arms race. I am not a pacifist in the sense of believing that military force should never be used. I would prefer to consider myself a rationalist who deplores the vanity and emotionalism that leads a nation to fight unnecessarily, or to arm to the teeth far beyond the necessities of defense or deterrence at colossal and debilitating cost, with the overkill serving no purpose but "prestige," which is nothing but a synonym for vanity.

Today, I come back to those two initial areas of my activity in foreign affairs because they still define the direction in which some hope would seem to lie. I have always seen the exchange program as a way to reinforce what the United Nations should ultimately be about, and vice versa. I have always coupled the two in my own thinking.

It is in these areas—education and international organization—more than in schemes of disarmament, that I discern the possibility of a hopeful future for humankind. I am not sure I would agree, even if we could, to a plan for getting rid of all the nuclear weapons. The world has gotten too complex for that. A system has to be designed for the preservation of deterrence not just between the superpowers but between them and other people. That is the ultimate sanction that we are not going to tolerate the continuation of aggression anywhere. And it is the underlying logic of the ABM treaty of 1972. Now the problem is, who is going to control these weapons? Proposals have been made for years. One such was the somewhat one-sided Baruch plan in the 1940s, which I think historians have since agreed was really designed to let the Americans retain a monopoly of control. No one is going to accept that anymore. Whether the U.N. Security Council could be entrusted with the control of the use of nuclear weapons is an open question, given how we view and work with the United Nations. Theoretically, it would be the best way to do it. But there is too much distrust to allow it now; it would take a lot of negotiations and confidence-building experience.

President Reagan professed to believe that we could get rid of these weapons altogether. That is not realistic. There will always be the danger that someone would have one that you don't know about, and while it might conceivably be possible to eliminate nuclear weapons, there is no conceivable way of eliminating the knowledge of how to make them. The basic principle of deterrence in the ABM treaty, which limited the Soviet Union and the United States to no more than one antimissile defense installation each, remains a sound one. It would make sense, however, to design some way of implementing this principle through the U.N. Security Council as the only available trustee of the whole human community. A small number of weapons is sufficient to accomplish such deterrence, as we have known from the beginning. Secretary of Defense Robert McNamara testified that four hundred intercontinental missiles were all you needed for such deterrence. The validity of his point has never been convincingly challenged. We need to cut back radically on all these weapons. But we also have to change the attitudes of the two superpowers towards them—towards their use and regulation.

In the long run, this cannot be accomplished without challenging one of the most destructive myths of the last two centuries: the myth of the sanctity of absolute national sovereignty. Our survival will depend on our capacity to develop at least some feelings of loyalty and responsibility to a larger political community than the nation-state. I know that creating an international community that might partially replace the old system is seen as a hopeless dream. But if it is truly hopeless, then the future of our species is in jeopardy. For it is the only viable, long-term alternative, the only course of realism and sanity. When the alternative to a long shot is no shot at all, then it is clear what the practical course of action is. We have no tried-and-true system to fall back on, only the constant reality of nuclear peril.

We have lived too long with these dreadful weapons; the danger of nuclear war now seems remote to many or most of us. The prospects of our disappearance as a species—or at least warnings thereof—have become something of a bore. But it is because we find the threat incredible that we go on in the same old traditional ways of conducting foreign affairs.

I recognize fully how very unfashionable it is these days to speak hopefully of the United Nations, and of the concept in which it is rooted, but I find no alternative. Given the rivalry between Russia and the United States and the proliferation of nuclear weapons, then logically, if there is any rationality left in the world, there would be a revival of interest in the United Nations and of meaningful negotiations toward making it work. In the past, neither superpower has taken the United Nations seriously. It has no strength of its own; it can only do what its major members in the Security Council wish it to do. If we do not give it money, if we do not support a peacekeeping force, it has no possibilities.

We supported the United Nations as long as we controlled the General Assembly. But when that control was lost with the proliferation of members following decolonization, we started to say the United Nations was of no use. We downgraded its reputation, and, in recent years, even refused to support it financially, as we are legally obligated to do. No doubt there was provocation in UNESCO, and there is no doubt that we are frequently subjected to provocative, insulting, and unrealistic statements in the General Assembly. But since Gorbachev in 1987 promised to pay the back dues owed by the Soviet Union and also suggested a more active role for the United Nations, it seems possible for us to reconsider the issue as well. President Reagan followed Gorbachev's example in 1988, promising to pay back dues owed by the United States. In the long run, it would be good politics as well as good policy for both of us to cooperate in and through the United Nations.

There is nothing much wrong with the U.N. machinery. The problem is simply that the major powers have been unwilling to entrust it with significant power and responsibility in the field of peacekeeping.

A standing U.N. force was contemplated and provided for in the Charter, but the major powers have never been willing to implement it. Neither the Russians nor the Americans, at present, would accept a militarily adequate, standing U.N. force composed of armed forces of small nations. But this is the way of the future, as an alternative to traditional warfare.

All of these great principles we talk about in the political field, whatever they mean in the abstract, have no practical meaning apart from the men and women who make the decisions to implement or nullify them. Very often it is only a few men and women who make the difference. In some countries it is just one. But even in our own country, with its widely disseminated democracy, there are always just a few. One or two people, often only the president, can make that difference in the final decision. Throughout history this has been true. Go back to the Greeks and the fatal decisions they made; the close decision that ruined Athens—that fatal expedition to Syracuse—

was essentially the product of a debate between two men, Nicias and Alcibiades. Had Nicias been more persuasive or Alcibiades less eloquent, a different history might have unfolded. Or consider the decisions that resulted in the outbreak of World War I. If the German leaders had been more rational, or the British more resolute, here too a different history might have unfolded. If those few people, I have often thought, in their respective countries, had had the experience of really knowing what the other countries involved were like, could have understood their motives and their background and their purposes, it would have made a great difference.

I have long been struck by the observation of Lord Grey, foreign secretary of Great Britain at the time of the outbreak of World War I, who wrote in his memoirs, "Nations are always making mistakes because they do not understand one another's psychology." They do not understand one another's purposes and motives and intentions. The superpowers today represent two great societies, both of them powerful, with diametrically opposed views of how to organize society, of how best to create the good life for their respective citizens. A deep antagonism arises out of the competition, and with it the age-old danger of nations "making mistakes because they do not understand one another's psychology." That is exactly what is at issue here. If Reagan and Gorbachev could each have spent a year in the other's country, lived and gone to school and interacted socially with the people, would it not have influenced them? Could it not have made a difference?

There is not much anyone can do to alter the *capacity* of these two nations to destroy each other. They have too much power, too many nuclear weapons and delivery systems, and, except for its ruinous costs, I do not think that continuing military escalation can have substantial effects—more fuel doesn't make much difference. On the other hand, it taxes the most optimistic imagination to contemplate the elimination of these weapons in the foreseeable future. We just change the ability of each side to destroy the other. What we can begin to change is the *attitudes* of the two sides.

I have long been an admirer of the views and writings of George Kennan, perhaps because he was the equivalent of a Fulbright scholar, having lived for so long in Moscow. He makes more sense than anyone else writing today about our relations. And when you look at the other people who lived there, Bohlen, for example, and contrast their views with others who did not, Acheson, Rusk, and Lovett, for example, I think that in almost every case I would see greater merit and insight in the views of the ones who lived there. They had a feeling about the Russians. Acheson was a brilliant man, but he didn't have any feeling for what the Russians were like; he simply mistrusted them.

From the beginning, my hope with the Fulbright exchanges was to generate a deeper understanding—especially on the part of potential leaders—of the differing cultures and peoples of the world. When scholars come here, it is not necessarily affection that they develop for us. Nor indeed do I think that that is one of its necessary purposes. It is quite enough if the exchange contributes to some feeling that there is a common humanity.

In the process, I hope that it will engender among those who come to the United States an understanding of what we are about and what we are like. I would hope, for example, that this understanding would enable those who come here and study here to look beyond rhetoric and therefore not to misinterpret our intentions and motives because of the character of our political debate.

The rhetoric in our free-wheeling democracy—from president to members of Congress to leading citizens—tends at times to be offensive and antagonistic to foreign listeners.

There is nothing one can or should do about such expressions—the cure would be worse than the disease—but our public references to certain foreign countries and peoples tend at times to be gratuitously offensive. Russians and Arabs are especially singled out—the former caricatured as clumsy and brutal but also diabolically clever, the latter stereotyped as "terrorists." As I mentioned, when I talked with President Nasser of Egypt in 1959, he was offended by the speeches in Congress and by other public officials. Foreign leaders do not always quite understand the freedom of speech in this country—and the excessive, irresponsible use to which it is sometimes put. We do understand it and we take a lot of it with a grain of salt, but foreigners who are not used to it in their own countries are puzzled and offended. This is one of many difficulties that educational exchange can help to overcome.

The idea for the exchanges came to me soon after the end of World War II. The dropping of the bombs on Hiroshima and Nagasaki in August 1945 gave rise to great apprehension about the implications of nuclear weapons for the shape and destiny of the postwar world. There were hearings in the Senate on the bomb and its implications, including testimony by nuclear scientists such as J. Robert Oppenheimer and Hans Bethe. Everyone was, to say the least, curious about these new weapons and what they might mean for the future of our country and of the world. Only a few people in Congress had known about their development; perhaps two or three members of the appropriations committees of the two houses had been apprised of the Manhattan Project. To most of us in Congress, the Hiroshima bomb was as great a surprise as it was to the general population.

The hearings on the bomb, held in the large Senate caucus room, were heavily attended. Their purpose was educational—to explain how the bomb worked and what it might mean for the future. I was impressed by its potential for destruction, as was everybody else. I was even more impressed by Einstein's portentous statement: that now everything had changed except our manner of thinking, and that if we did not change our thinking about the world and our place in it, we would soon enough be faced with incalculable catastrophe.

What could we do to translate historical portent into practical action—and do before the impulse to innovate atrophied? Surely something ought to be done. Everybody was against war in 1945; we were conscious of its destructive waste in a way that must seem innocent and naïve to the present generation—a generation that has had limited experience of war and none of global war. But how long would the feeling that it was necessary and possible to reshape the world last? It was a question of developing something that practical politicians would be willing to do, but that would also have significance and long-term consequences. The United Nations was our main hope, and I supported it strongly, as I still do. But my thoughts turned too to the possibilities of international education.

Receiving a Rhodes scholarship had undoubtedly altered my life in numerous ways. Getting one came like a bolt out of the blue. It had never occurred to me as an available opportunity. I grew up in Fayetteville, Arkansas, a small Ozark Mountain town of about eight or ten thousand inhabitants. My family moved there from Missouri when I was about a year old. I lived there until 1925, when I went to Oxford. It was a very serene place, home of the University of Arkansas. My schooling was always a part of that university, from the time I entered the Peabody training school on the university campus to graduation from the university in 1925. Until then, I had not ventured very often or very far from Arkansas. I had never thought about going away to school, even in the United States, until one day my former English professor stopped me. We were old friends, and he said he had received the forms to apply for the Rhodes scholarship. I don't think I'd ever heard of it. He explained what you do and asked if I would like to apply, and I said, "Well, sure."

So I did. In those days Rhodes scholars were selected on a state basis rather than from regions in the United States. There was a state committee composed of former Rhodes scholars. I went to Little Rock—all the state applicants did—to be interviewed. There were seven or eight others. There was an oral examination, which consisted of general questions about your attitude towards life and what you had done in the university and elsewhere.

The qualifications for the Rhodes include your academic work, but that is not decisive. They also include athletic ability, which Rhodes describes in his will as evidence of manliness and evidence of your potential for leadership. I happened to have been active in the organization of the first student government at the University of Arkansas. I was also active as a member of the Sigma Chi fraternity, although I lived at home. I was considered to be a good football player, although in those days it was a much simpler, more amateur college sport than it is today. That was probably the decisive difference between my record and the others'.

Oxford was a new and strange world for me, as well as a great cultural shock. Shortly after I arrived, I made the Oxford-Cambridge lacrosse team. I played rugby football for the college. In Oxford athletics is even more admired in a sense than in an American college. If you play games well, you are invited into the literary and social clubs. They think that if you play games well you are a gentleman—someone to be accepted—so I was invited into various clubs and societies.

The intellectual sophistication of these young Englishmen astonished me. I was embarrassed by my own inadequacy. The literary clubs met once a month to present papers on prominent authors. I was astonished by the intellectual maturity of those seventeen- and eighteen-year-old boys. So I began to read seriously. The first paper I ever wrote was on Sherwood Anderson. I thought it would be appropriate to take an American author.

I didn't know much about him until I prepared that paper. But I worked very hard on the paper. I never had taken my education so seriously before I came under the peer pressure from those English boys, because it was humiliating to be so inadequate in comparison to one's contemporaries. So, I seriously began to read and become a little more knowledgeable, and I concentrated on history.

R. B. McCallum was the young don who became my tutor. He couldn't have been more sympathetic and understanding. His main criticism of my weekly papers usually was my use of the English language, the parochialism of my language. I used words that were quite customary at home, but he didn't think they were acceptable. In every direction I turned, I became conscious of my intellectual backwardness. McCallum was an admirer of Woodrow Wilson and undoubtedly influenced my ideas, as did the years of foreign travel that began when I went to Oxford. It's not easy to say quite how, but I am sure all this influenced my later ideas on the Fulbright exchange program, and the kind of significance it could have on the attitudes of individuals interacting with different cultures.

One afternoon in September 1945, after the destruction of Hiroshima and Nagasaki, I was at a tea party with Oscar Cox and Herbert Ellison in the home of a neighbor. Ellison, a sophisticated Englishman with a deep interest in international affairs, was then an editor of the *Washington Post.* Cox was a leading Washington lawyer with whom I had become ac-

quainted during the hearings in 1943 in the House of Representatives on Lend-Lease; he had accompanied Dean Acheson
in presenting the case for Lend-Lease. I brought up the idea
of establishing an educational exchange program. Having
been a Rhodes scholar, I naturally thought of that, and I was
also aware of the Boxer indemnity experience at the beginning of the century, when the Chinese reparations were
turned into an educational fund for Chinese students in this
country. There was also the precedent of the Belgian-Ameri-
can Foundation established after World War I.

Ellison and Cox were enthusiastic and supportive, and I was
gratified by their enthusiasm. But I also felt that if I were at
that time to emphasize what I believed and still believe to be
the real value of the Fulbright scholarships—which is their
contribution to the advancement of world peace and international community—the argument would not sell. I was casting
about for what is now called a "soft sell."

As first conceived, the proposal was an independent bill to
provide for the establishment of educational exchanges and
the authority to establish foundations for this purpose. As it
happened, however, there was also a bill before the Senate
Armed Services Committee, providing for the disposal of supplies left by our armed forces in various parts of the world.
You can imagine the extent of those supplies in all the places
where the American military had been operating. There were
assets in all of the western European countries and in much
of the rest of the world as well, including vast stores of such
things as trucks, food, drugs, and blankets—all the things a
modern army requires. Under the war-properties disposal bill,
the secretary of state was to be given authority to dispose of
assets held outside the United States, and to take foreign
credits for them, because none of the countries involved had
dollars to pay for them. Our principal allies owed us more
money than they could possibly pay, and they had no dollars

and no access to dollars. So it was a question of taking IOUs or nonconvertible credits in payment.

So I thought, why not use such credits for the educational program? It was, in my view, quite improbable, virtually impossible, to obtain any appropriations for such a cultural purpose at that time. The Congress was not accustomed to supporting cultural activities, even domestically. This was before there was any federal aid to education other than very limited vocational programs and the old Land Grant Colleges Act dating from Lincoln's time. Therefore, as a practical matter, I focused on the idea of applying the foreign credits to educational exchange—the selling point being, as far as my colleagues were concerned, that it would not require appropriations from the Treasury.

I did some research and talked about the idea in private. I wrote to ex-President Hoover, the memory of whose effective relief work after World War I lent weight to his support, and received from him a fine letter endorsing the idea. I talked to people in the National Educational Association and in the American Council of Learned Societies. Hearings were held in early 1946 in the subcommittee of the Senate Armed Services Committee that had jurisdiction over war-properties disposal. Senator Joseph O'Mahoney of Wyoming—a remarkably intelligent and educated man—happened to be chairman. That was a very happy coincidence. I doubt that any other member of the Senate would have been as understanding and cooperative. I testified, offering the Hoover letter and the relative precedents in support, and various other people, including Bill Benton—then an assistant secretary of state, later a senator from Connecticut—gave helpful testimony as well.

The committee voted out the bill, and it then faced passage in the full Senate. I knew that it wasn't the kind of bill with which you wanted to arouse members' suspicions. It could

211

pass only if it could get through without debate, as quietly as possible. I still think that was true. There were too many people suspicious of such a program—people who didn't want American youth corrupted by foreign "isms."

The majority leader agreed to support the bill, and I then approached the minority leader. The Senate has what is called the unanimous-consent calendar, and the minority usually has a couple of people assigned to monitor it so that they will not be surprised by the bills that are expected to come up. Most such bills are routine. The educational exchange was certainly not, in my judgment, a routine bill. Nonetheless it did not involve a large amount of money, and that was one of the criteria of whether it was an important bill or not. It involved no American tax money and it required no authorization for appropriations. It was merely an allocation of nonconvertible currencies or credits, and therefore, under normal Senate procedure, a routine matter.

So I went to the Republican minority leader, Senator Kenneth Wherry of Nebraska. I emphasized to him that the proposal was not going to be a drain on the Treasury. I also recalled our experience with World War I debts, in which, after years of acrimony and ill will, we didn't get very much back. Other than Finland's debt, which was paid, payments were suspended under the Hoover moratorium of the Depression years, and then, when payments were to be resumed, all the major debtors defaulted. So I argued that we had a good opportunity to get something out of these credits, whereas before, we had gotten nothing, and in this way persuaded the Republican leadership not to oppose the bill when it came up on the calendar.

When it came up on the Senate floor, I didn't say much. In order to avoid possible controversy, I was very brief, and since the Armed Services Committee had approved the bill, it went through without debate. Later, when Senator McKellar of

Tennessee found out about it, he said that if he had been aware of the issue, he would have objected because it was a very dangerous thing to send our fine young men and women abroad to be exposed to those foreign "isms." He meant it. He thought it was dangerous to expose young Americans to countries whose governments advocated socialism, communism, or any alternative to our American way. If I had made a major speech on the bill and had speculated on its possibilities as I contemplated them, or if the issue had been taken up by the press at the time, somebody probably would have objected. And one objection was all that was needed to prevent passage. I doubt that it would have gotten through if it had come to a full debate.

As it turned out, the bill passed unanimously, with no roll-call, under the unanimous-consent procedure: "Any objection? No objection. Passed." It was done at about 5:30 in the afternoon. There was nobody on the floor except those four or five who had come with me. That's the way you get good bills through the Senate.

In the House, where the bill had to go next, Congressman Will Whittington was just the opposite of O'Mahoney. A senior member of the House from Mississippi, and chairman of the comparable subcommittee in the House, he was very suspicious of the whole idea. And he said to me, "I want to examine this bill." He thought I was an upstart, a little young and inexperienced to be messing around with legislation. I ought to be quiet and defer to my elders. I tried to explain that these credits were not convertible into dollars, and were not usable in America, and that it didn't entail appropriations. I don't think I ever made the case. I didn't convey credibility. He just didn't believe me, I think, so he didn't find time to look into the bill. He just wasn't going to do anything. He just sat on it.

I thought I had lost. And then one day I was having lunch

with the undersecretary of state, Will Clayton from Texas. He was a prominent cotton man, the founder of the Anderson-Clayton Cotton Company, and a very sophisticated man. He did business all over the world. He was a real diplomat in many ways. I explained the situation to him. He approved of the idea of the exchange and said that, by coincidence, he had done business as a young man in the same community that Will Whittington represented, and knew him from way back. He said he would speak to him. He did, and he persuaded him to let the bill go through. The difference was that Whittington believed Will Clayton, as he evidently had not believed me, when Clayton told him that these credits could not be used in Mississippi or anywhere else in this country. That made the difference and the bill went through the House. It just barely got through in time to be signed on August 1, 1946, before Congress recessed. If it had not been approved then, I doubt it would have gotten through later. The timing was just as close as could be.

The next hazard was the question of the bill's constitutionality—the issue being whether there was authority to allocate funds without an appropriation. The question was submitted to the attorney general for a ruling. It took about six months to get the decision that it was constitutional because the credits involved did not qualify as funds in the Treasury under the Constitution. That was a technical, but troublesome, detail and the decision was fortunate.

Those first few years of organizing the program were very interesting for me. The legislation had provided for the creation of a Board of Foreign Scholarships as the policy-making body, so as to insulate the selection procedure from the risk of political interference. I was invited informally to go to the initial meetings of the board. It was Bill Benton who spoke of the program to the press at this time as the "Fulbright program"—at the first press conference in which the program was explained. From that time on, the press referred to it this way.

I had not wanted this to be solely an American program. In each country, binational commissions were to develop the kind of program that made sense to them—what kinds of students, or teachers and professors, should be selected, what kind of research work. The binational commissions would make their recommendations to the Board of Foreign Scholarships, which had the final authority, but the commissions' recommendations were usually followed. In later years, Indira Gandhi made the statement that the program was a form of cultural imperialism, that we were imposing our cultural ideas upon them. The charge was inaccurate: the binational commissions and the way they have been administered have protected the program against political and cultural bias.

As early as 1948 some foreign credits were being exhausted, and Congress adopted an amendment to legislation known as the Smith-Mundt Act to authorize appropriations for the exchange program. By 1961, the program had grown so substantial that new sources of funding were required. The foreign credits from the war had been exhausted in all but a few countries; if the program was to survive and develop further, appropriations would be required. For this purpose the legislation had to be handled in the customary way—no more unanimous consent.

I asked Representative Wayne Hayes, a member of the House Foreign Affairs Committee, to introduce a new bill in the House and to join as co-sponsor, as he did. I asked him rather than the chairman of the Foreign Affairs Committee because Wayne was head of what is commonly called the "housekeeping committee" of the House, and in that capacity had acquired great influence with the members. The housekeeping committee distributes perquisites to House members, such as offices and allowances; its chairman is accordingly influential. Hayes had not previously been identified with the program, but after he became a co-sponsor and was recognized as a friend by the educators of the country, he was more active in his support of the program.

A major problem with a program like this one, which arose in the early days, is that it has little appeal to members of Congress. Relatively little money was involved, and until recently it had only a small constituency. Today it has developed a much larger constituency and has received good support from Congress during recent years. Previously, although the program readily elicited praise, it was praise without commitment, except on the part of those few who actually participated in its activities.

Another problem that arose in connection with the program, which I had not anticipated, was the problem of "brain drain." On one occasion the ambassador of Pakistan came to see me and said in effect, "Look, we know that you meant well with this program, but what is happening is that you get some of our best young people, especially in the fields of medicine and science. They come here and then they don't want to go back to Pakistan, because the opportunities here, for both research and practice, are so much greater. We can't go on like that; it's taking some of our best brains."

So we agreed that it would help to change the rules: thereafter anyone who accepted a Fulbright grant—both American students studying abroad and foreign students studying here—would have to leave the country in which he or she had studied for at least two years. They would presumably go home, although we could not require that. They might go to France or England, but they could not remain here. That provision was passed and became part of the law. It was an effort in the program to deal with the "brain drain."

It is especially unfortunate that the Soviet Union is not a major participant in the exchange program. In the early 1970s, I had a conversation with Madame Kruglova, who represented the Soviet ministry of cultural affairs, in which we discussed the possibility of applying part of the outstanding World War II Lend-Lease account that the Soviets had agreed to repay to Fulbright fellowships. They had agreed at that time to pay about $800 million worth of the Lend-Lease account. This represented a compromise settlement of several billions. I wanted to get part of that, maybe a hundred million, for exchange with Russia. It would have been a great thing.

She thought the proposal was interesting and said that she would take it back for discussions with her government. All it would have entailed was an agreement to use a designated amount for exchanges. That would have been to the Soviets' advantage because they could pay the agreed amount in rubles instead of dollars and thus save themselves the hard currency. Most unfortunately, it all fell through when the Jackson amendment aborted key elements of the Nixon détente. The Soviets abrogated the trade agreement in retaliation, and down the drain with it went the Lend-Lease settlement and all the other joint ventures. Although the two countries pursued space collaboration a little longer, the Jackson amendment—as I have no doubt it was intended to do—took all the heart out of the détente movement.

The essence of intercultural education is the acquisition of empathy—the ability to see the world as others see it, and to allow for the possibility that others may see something that we have failed to see, or may see it more accurately. That, I should think, is the most pressing necessity in superpower relations. This is not to suggest that if Americans and Russians

217

really knew each other better all animosity and rivalry would disappear. It hardly needs emphasis that we in the Western democratic tradition will continue to deplore the harshness, the secretiveness, the suppression of ideas, and the denial of personal freedom that characterize authoritarian societies, both communist and noncommunist.

Total approval, however, is not what empathy requires. What it does require—applied to Russia, for example—is an appreciation of the deep-seated fear, rooted in a harsh and tragic history, that the Russians feel for their borders and their security. As a wise and experienced American diplomat, who served in the U.S. Embassy in Moscow in the 1970s and early 1980s, observed, "In order to live in peace with the Russians, Americans must stop denying them the right to their own view of reality. Russian political culture reflects Russian history and embodies what the Russian people, mistakenly or not, believe is necessary for their survival."*

Americans, it has been said, cannot remember what other countries cannot forget. The United States is one of the very few major countries that have never had what to my mind is the highly educational if tragic experience of being invaded and occupied by a hostile army. On our two borders are two friendly and militarily weak nations. In contrast, the Russian steppes have been, throughout history, tempting invasion routes to foreign aggressors, who, since the thirteenth century, have succumbed to that temptation on numerous occasions. We should recognize that these experiences have affected and do affect the Soviets' point of view.

The simple, basic purpose of the exchange program we initiated over forty years ago is to erode the culturally rooted mistrust that sets nations against one another. Its essential

*John M. Joyce, "The Old Russian Legacy," *Foreign Policy* (Summer 1984), p. 152.

aim is to encourage people in all countries, and especially their political leaders, to stop denying others the right to their own view of reality and to develop a new manner of thinking about how to avoid war rather than to wage it. The exchange program is not a panacea but an avenue of hope—possibly our best hope and conceivably our only hope—for the survival and further progress of humanity.

AFTERWORD:

ON CHANGING OUR MANNER OF THINKING

I f it were possible to summarize the meaning of the history of the world since World War II in a single sentence, the words spoken by Albert Einstein on the occasion of the Hiroshima bomb might come close. "Now," he said, "everything has changed except our manner of thinking."

Most of us know, in our minds if not in our hearts, that the world has indeed changed. We know that this human species, which through eons of time evolved to become masters of the earth, have now acquired the capacity to destroy the earth, or at least to destroy most of the vestiges of civilized life upon the earth. Oddly enough—or perhaps not so oddly—some of our military leaders have been in the forefront among those who have tried to warn us of the probable consequences of an all-out nuclear war. Speaking to a congressional committee in 1981, the chairman of the Joint Chiefs of Staff, General David Jones, warned of casualties in the hundreds of millions, amounting overall to "the greatest catastrophe in history by many orders of magnitude." Another distinguished general, Dwight Eisenhower, commented in 1953, the first year of his presidency, that in the nuclear age "the only thing worse than losing a global war was winning one." He asked, "What would we do with Russia if we should win a global war?"

There have been many such warnings over the years, including the warning of scientists like Carl Sagan, who has calculated the likelihood of climatic catastrophe in the form of

223

a deadly nuclear winter if warheads beyond a threshold of 500 to 2,000 are simultaneously fired off.

What is perhaps more remarkable—and more ominous—than these apocalyptic projections is how little attention we pay to them. Experts may quibble over whether Carl Sagan's threshold for climatic catastrophe is too low by a few hundred warheads, but no rational person to my knowledge would contest the proposition that an all-out nuclear war would indeed be "the greatest catastrophe in history by many orders of magnitude." Nevertheless, we continue to conduct our international relations in the same old way—by the same rules of crisis management, balance of power, arms races, and confrontation that always in the past—not sometimes but always—have sooner or later culminated in war. We still base our policies on Clausewitz's formula, that war is an extension of politics, carried out "by other means," and not on President Kennedy's proposition, expressed in his inaugural address in 1961, that war "can no longer serve to settle disputes" because if we do not put an end to it, it will put an end to us. Everything has indeed changed, and we readily acknowledge it—but not to the point that it has significantly changed our manner of thinking.

I do not suggest that there has been no progress, or that there is no hope for the future. For over forty years the superpowers have kept the precarious peace under conditions that likely would have led to war in the prenuclear age. The balance of terror has supplanted the old balance of power and so far it has worked—at least to the extent of restraining the superpowers from suicidal conflict.

But terror alone is a dubious, fragile foundation on which to rest our hopes for the future peace and progress of mankind. At best it serves as a kind of holding action—against the time when more civilized impulses will govern our *thinking* and shape our behavior. Back in 1932, Sigmund Freud, in response to an inquiry from Albert Einstein, ventured the prediction that two factors—"man's cultural disposition" and "a well-founded dread of the form that future wars will take"—might someday put an end to war between nations. Thus far in the nuclear age it has been the latter—that "well-founded dread"—that has kept the nuclear peace, rather than progress in our cultural disposition. The superpowers have continued to compete, in the age-old manner of great and powerful nations, to establish the supremacy of one or the other—or as President Nixon used to say, we want to show the world that America is still number one. Instead of going to war with each other, we have waged the conflict through proxies—in Vietnam and Afghanistan, in the Middle East and Central America—and through an economically debilitating arms race. The methods have been modified but the objectives by and large have not.

I say "by and large" because recent and prospective events—such as the INF treaty and the upcoming Moscow summit—provide basis for hope that we may at last be moving in a new direction. It is too soon to offer confident predictions, but there are some indications—to which I will return—that Soviet and American leaders are beginning to recognize the destructive futility of the arms race and are beginning to see some advantages in cooperation, or if not in cooperation, then in more peaceful, productive forms of competition.

There is nothing wrong with competition as such, or with the ambition to be number one. It depends what you are competing for, or what you want to be number one *at*. There is the harmless, more or less enjoyable competition of a golf match or pennant race or superbowl. There is the achievement in science or literature or the arts. And there is, or can be, a productive competition between societies—in education, economic productivity, or social services—in all the diverse activities that make a better life for the people.

For my own part I am convinced that our relative success to date in competing with the Russians for the allegiance of countries of the third world has much more to do with the freedom and abundance of our society than with arms sales or proxy wars or our clumsy effort at subverting or destabilizing regimes we dislike, such as the Sandinistas in Nicaragua. Tens of thousands of students from all over the world—including the most populous communist country, China—come to the United States rather than the Soviet Union to study because of the quality and diversity of our educational institutions, because of the freedom of intellectual exchange, and, I strongly suspect, because life in general is more interesting and stimulating in America than it is in Russia.

Interestingly enough, some thirty years ago the Soviet Union leader Nikita Khrushchev challenged us to a competition on exactly those grounds where *we* have the advantage. I had the privilege of hosting Khrushchev at a meeting of the Senate Foreign Relations Committee on September 16, 1959. On that occasion he expressed both envy and admiration for America's economic progress and invited us to join in a competition to see whose system could make a better life for the people. "I should say," he said, "that future generations would be grateful to us if we managed to switch our efforts from stockpiling and perfecting weapons and concentrated those efforts fully on competition in the economic field."

I think we should have accepted that challenge then, and I think we should accept it now as reiterated by General Secretary Gorbachev. We have experienced over the last thirty years, since Khrushchev issued his challenge, alternating periods of détente and cold war—halting, tentative initiatives for arms control, trade, and culture exchange, followed by renewed arms races and proxy conflicts. We went from Eisenhower's "spirit of Geneva" to the Cuban missile crisis, from Kennedy's nuclear-test-ban treaty to the Vietnam War, from the Nixon-Kissinger détente of the early 1970s to President Reagan's campaign against the "evil empire." There were many complex reasons for the failures and setbacks of détente, but at bottom, I believe, was the inability or unwillingness of both Russians and Americans, at critical junctures, to change their manner of thinking.

If we cannot change our manner of thinking about the world and its problems, and if the struggle continues as it has in the past, both superpowers are likely to be losers. Walter Lippmann pointed out many years ago that an essential element of any nation's foreign policy is its solvency. For over forty years we have been sustaining the arms race and our global commitments by neglecting our domestic base and, for the last seven years, by spending radically beyond our means. It is fairly obvious that when you draw down your capital over a long period—the domestic infrastructure of education, health, the environment, and productive investment—it will eventually and inevitably take its toll on the nation's security and ability to act in foreign affairs, as well as on the well-being of our people. Despite differences, there are striking similarities in the conditions of the Soviet Union and the United States. Military costs drain the human and financial resources of both countries. The Soviet economy is stagnant and unproductive while ours appears to be booming—but the boom is based on budget deficits and borrowed foreign money. We are living well today by mortgaging our children's future. Neither the Soviet nor the American economy is solvent. And neither superpower is much of a model or magnet anymore for the

227

emerging nations of the third world. The Marxist god has failed—but is America still the model for humankind, that "city upon a hill" that John Winthrop foresaw in 1630?

On September 12, 1821, Thomas Jefferson wrote a letter to John Adams in which he said that "the flames kindled on the 4th of July, 1776, have spread over too much of the globe to be extinguished by the feeble engines of despotism; on the contrary, they will consume those engines and all who work them." Those flames, it now appears, have dimmed. New dynamic and magnetic forces have arisen in the world. They are to be found in such places as western Europe and Japan and those "tigers" of productive growth, the newly industrialized countries of Asia. These are what we might call the "civilian" great powers of the nuclear age. Germany and Japan in particular have learned the lessons and paid the price of military adventure, and they have found a better way.

I am not of the Spenglerian school that says that nations are foreordained to rise and fall according to some cosmic plan. The only predestiny there is in human affairs is the predestiny locked within us—the tendency to persist in the patterns of the past, to repeat the mistakes of our ancestors, to persist beyond reason and utility in old, discredited manners of thinking.

In other words, I think we are the authors of our own future. We study the past not to discover our destiny but to master it, to gain hints and perspectives and insights on how we can improve upon the performance of our ancestors. I would go further and say that I think there is a reasonable chance we are going to succeed. Both recent events and current prospects suggest that we may be moving in the direction of peaceful competition with the Soviets—and even more important, toward real cooperation for a lasting peace.

I am encouraged that the same president who a few years

ago was railing against the "evil empire" is now the stalwart advocate of the intermediate-range nuclear-missiles treaty. The same president who in his first news conference on coming to office in 1981 proclaimed that the leaders of the Soviet Union "reserve unto themselves the right to commit any crime, to lie, to cheat" to advance their cause, now applauds the changes that have taken place in Russia under Gorbachev, says that better relations between the Soviet Union and the United States are "absolutely essential," and even acknowledges that we have some unresolved problems such as homelessness in the United States. The trouble is that it took seven years to educate him and in another few months we may have to start the process all over again—but that is another matter.

I am equally encouraged by the progress made by Mikhail Gorbachev through his policies of *glasnost* and *perestroika.* I do not suppose for a moment that Gorbachev plans to turn the Soviet Union into a western-style democracy. I am not sure that would be a good thing for Russia, in the light of its history and political culture. But that in any event is not our concern, because, as noted, the Russians have the right to their own view of reality.

What is our concern is the new, positive Soviet attitude on arms control and trade, on cultural exchange and strengthening the United Nations. In September 1987 General Secretary Gorbachev made a most remarkable proposal for expanding the authority of the United Nations by giving the Security Council real authority to enforce peace and verify arms-control agreements, giving the World Court mandatory jurisdiction, creating a UN tribunal to investigate acts of terrorism, creating a world space organization, and increasing the authority of the Atomic Energy Agency. Then in October 1987 the Soviet Union announced that it would pay all its outstanding debts to the United Nations, including $197 million owed since 1973 for Middle East peacekeeping operations.

I would hope that the United States would follow suit, first by paying its own debts to the United Nations, next by engaging the Soviet Union and other countries in a dialogue on the means of implementing Gorbachev's proposals for strengthening the United Nations. I would hope too that we might join with the Russians in other joint ventures—in such fields as medical research, energy research, protection of the global environment, and space exploration. The Soviets have expressed interest in a joint manned mission to Mars. I personally would not place that at the top of the agenda—I would rather start with education, the environment, and homelessness in America and poverty in the Third World—but if we must go to Mars, then let us by all means go together.

Joint ventures, aside from their intrinsic value, have the added, perhaps greater value of alleviating mistrust. Men and women who work together to solve a problem or reach a common goal often develop a sense of comradeship and trust; they become humanized in each other's eyes. To many Americans the Soviets remain an abstraction—an evil abstraction embodying a feared and alien ideology—and to many Russians, no doubt, we appear the same, in a kind of mirror image. I do not expect that the ideologies of Russia and the West will soon be reconciled, nor is it especially important that they ever be reconciled. The Soviets may hold their view of reality, while we hold—and cherish—our own. What is important is that we come to think about each other as human beings. We do not have to admire the Soviet system to allow of the possibility that the Soviet leaders, like our own, genuinely fear for their nation's security. Nor is it wholly unreasonable to believe that the Soviet people share the usual aspirations of other peoples for the good life, for good food and shelter, for all the amenities that make life interesting and fulfilling and that ensure a hopeful future for their children.

Of all the joint ventures in which we might engage, the most productive, in my view, is educational exchange. I have always had great difficulty—since the initiation of the Fulbright scholarships in 1946—in trying to find the words that would persuasively explain that educational exchange is not merely one of those nice but marginal activities in which we engage in international affairs, but rather, from the standpoint of future world peace and order, probably the most important and potentially rewarding of our foreign-policy activities.

There is a multiplier effect in international education and it carries the possibility—the only real possibility—of changing our manner of thinking about the world, and therefore of changing the world. For every university professor whose outlook has been broadened by study in another country, many thousands of students will gain some measure of intercultural perspective. For every business person who has studied in another country, many associates are likely to gain some appreciation of the essential futility of nationalistic economic policies and of the way in which an international division of labor benefits all countries. For every politician or diplomat who, through study abroad, has gained some appreciation of the world as a human community, untold numbers of ordinary citizens, as well as their leaders, may be guided away from parochialism and narrow nationalism to broader, more fruitful perspectives.

I think it quite likely, for example, that General Secretary Gorbachev has a more realistic perspective on the United States than he might otherwise have because of the advice he receives from Anatoly Dobrynin, who served as ambassador in the United States for many years and knows our country intimately, and from Alexander Yakovlev, who studied in the United States as a Fulbright scholar in the 1950s.

The first requirement is leadership—a new kind of leadership committed to a new manner of thinking. From ancient

231

times to the present, the most esteemed leaders have been war leaders, many of them warriors themselves, celebrated for their heroic deeds as in the ancient world, more commonly for heroic rhetoric in the modern world. Many were indeed great leaders, like Churchill, who through eloquence and force of character inspired the British people to stand against Hitler's onslaught. But by contrast, what was so great about Alexander the Great, who contributed little to the culture, politics, or religion of the ancient world, whose legacy was one of conquest, destruction, self-aggrandizement, and savagery?

The age of warrior kings and of warrior presidents has passed. The nuclear age calls for a different kind of leadership—a leadership of intellect, judgment, tolerance, and rationality, a leadership committed to human values, to world peace, and to the improvement of the human condition.

Today we need a leadership that recognizes that the fundamental challenge in this nuclear hi-tech era is one of psychology and education in the field of human relations. It is not the kind of problem that is likely to be resolved by expertise—even the sophisticated expertise of our most gifted military thinkers, who delight in exotic weapon systems and strategic doctrines that threaten the solvency of the richest nations as well as their physical survival. The attributes upon which we must draw are the human attributes of compassion and common sense, of intellect and creative imagination, and of empathy and understanding between cultures. As Abraham Lincoln put it in his second annual message to Congress, during the worst days of the Civil War, "As our case is new, so we must think anew and act anew. We must disenthrall ourselves, and then we shall save our country."

Index

J. William Fulbright was one of the most distinguished and influential senators of our time. He represented Arkansas in the U.S. Senate from 1945 to 1974, during which time he chaired the Foreign Relations Committee longer than any senator in American history. Since 1975 he has been counsel at the Washington law firm Hogan and Hartson, and is author of many notable books, including *The Arrogance of Power, The Crippled Giant,* and *Old Myths and New Realities.*

Seth P. Tillman is research professor of diplomacy at Georgetown University. He was a long-term member of the professional staff of the Senate Foreign Relations Committee. Tillman is the author of *The United States in the Middle East: Interests and Obstacles* and *Anglo-American Relations and the Paris Peace Conference of 1919.*